PIMPIN'

from the

Pulpit

to the

PEWS

Exposing & Expelling The Spirit
Of Lust In The Church

PIMPIN'

from the

Pulpit

to the

PEWS

Exposing & Expelling The Spirit
Of Lust In The Church

Hasani Pettiford

Hasani Pettiford Publications
West Orange, New Jersey

Hasani Pettiford is available for speaking engagements. Contact the office or send an email to info@hasani.com

PIMPIN' From The Pulpit To The Pews

Cover Design by:
Vizuri Graphics – Danielle Pettiford

Editor:
Shirley Pettiford

Library of Congress Catalog Card Number: 2003106107
ISBN: 0-9707915-1-8

HASANI PETTIFORD PUBLICATIONS
534 Mt. Pleasant Avenue
West Orange, New Jersey 07052
Phone (973)676-4125 * Fax (973) 736-8130
www.hasani.com

Discounts on this book are available for bulk purchases. Write or call for information on our discount programs.

CONTENTS

INTRODUCTION

Ephesians 5:11 says, "Take no part in the unfruitful works of darkness, but instead expose them." This powerful passage of scripture is more than just a quotable verse hidden within a vast realm of scriptural content, but a charge to live by. I've spent eight years of my life traveling across the nation to university campuses teaching students the importance of godly relationships and sexual purity.

The typical college campus has transformed from an institution of higher learning to an underworld of erotic lust and sexual showdowns. Lust and sexual self-gratification have become the core curriculum. There is a tremendous pressure in college to live a promiscuous life. Unfortunately, many students regard sex as an extra-curricular activity – nothing more, nothing less. My deep concern and gross disgust for the present day sexual/relational state of affairs birthed the book *Black Thighs, Black Guys & Bedroom Lies*.

While on tour, I've met countless individuals in the church who have regretfully experienced the same sexual games and bedroom lies discussed in the book. Fornication, adultery, masturbation, homosexuality, promiscuity, pornography, and other sexual strongholds have crept into the pulpits, altars and pews of the church. The spirit of lust has consumed the lives of many

Christians. How? Lust is not a respecter of persons. While many run into prayer lines seeking deliverance from sexual sin, they often find themselves right back into what they've just gotten out of. Rather than overcoming the internal struggle between the flesh and the spirit, many are encouraged to rush to the altar and marry to avoid 'burning'. Unfortunately, most Christians have not been taught how to effectively pursue sexual purity.

PIMPIN' From The Pulpit To The Pews: Exposing & Expelling The Spirit Of Lust In The Church is a comprehensive look inside the church suffering from the spirit of lust. The Apostle Paul wrote letters to the church warning them about the dangers of sexual immorality and encouraging them to live righteous lives. The same burden that Paul had, to help the church in the area of sexual purity, has been placed upon me as well. This seven-chapter book is a letter to the church that takes the reader on a spiritual journey from sexual sin to a lifestyle of sexual purity. Each chapter offers an inside look into a specific area, within the body of Christ, that the spirit of lust has affected.

Chapter one, There's A Spirit In The House, offers an overview of the spiritual/carnal state of affairs within the church. It explores how the spirit of lust has entered into the church through the practice of Baal worship. Married, single, young and adult Christians struggle with this lustful spirit, which has manifested itself in various forms of sexual misconduct which have served to destroy the church.

Chapter two, The Power Of A Preying Preacher, focuses on how sexual sin has entered into the ranks of clergy. It explains how carnal clergy use their title, power and position to sexually prey on unsuspecting members within the church. The chapter also explores the insatiable infatuation that wayward parishioners have for those who serve in ministry. It concludes with an admonishment for the wrong that has been done and a path towards restoration for those within ministry that have fallen astray.

Chapter three, *The Secret Underworld Of Homosexuality In The Church,* is an eye opener to the overwhelming presence of the homosexual (gay, lesbian and bisexual) lifestyle in the church. The chapter challenges the 'Gay Theology' that homosexuals use to justify their lifestyle. It concludes by offering hope for the future and a path for deliverance.

Chapter four, *Teen Sexuality: Is There A Virgin In The House?* exposes the shocking reality of the sexual promiscuity that runs amuck in both public and Christian school systems across the nation. It explains how Satan's five-fold ministry has trapped young people in a world of pornography and forbidden sexual exploration. The chapter ends by explaining the consequences of sexual sin and the benefits of preserving virginity until marriage.

Chapter five, *Overcoming The Lust Of The Eyes,* shares biblical accounts of men and women who have fallen from God's grace and suffered severe consequences because of the lust of the eyes. It offers practical steps for controlling the eyes of man. Singles are taught to keep their eyes upon the Lord and married couples are taught to keep their eyes on each other.

Chapter six, *Help: My Body's Yearnin' & My Flesh Is Burnin'!* is entirely dedicated to the individual struggle of sexual sin. It tackles the controversial topic of masturbation, as well as, the secret thought life and the eternal struggle between the flesh and the spirit. It concludes by offering practical steps that Christians must take in order to completely overcome and destroy the spirit of lust in their lives.

Chapter seven, *Killing The Spirit In The House,* provides a scriptural blueprint of what must be done to remove the spirit of lust from both the church and the lives of its members. It explains the importance of establishing a ministry of sex education within the church. The chapter brings closure to the book by explaining what the spiritual status of every Christian should be lead on a daily basis.

As you read this book some of you may question my qualifications for writing on such a topic. Well, I have no degree from any seminary or theological school, no formal ministerial training or any group of letters that appear at the end of my name that would warrant me an expert on such a topic. The only qualification I have is my own personal testimony and the call from God to go out into the world and teach the Gospel of Jesus Christ.

The ministry of relationships and sexual purity is the grace that God has put upon my life. Why? It's simple. You cannot heal what you cannot feel. Hebrews 4:15 says *"For we have not an high priest which cannot be touched with the feeling of our infirmities; but was in all points tempted like as we are, yet without sin."* Unfortunately, I cannot profess to be without sin but I am able to sympathize with the weaknesses and sexual temptations of others.

I know what it's like to grow up in the church and be taught the do and don'ts of Christian living. I know what it's like to maintain virginity all throughout my teen years into the age of maturity. I know what it's like to travel from state to state and have an assortment of sexually aggressive women show up at my hotel room in the middle of the night seeking more than a lecture, as well as women who obtain keys of their own in order to crawl in between the sheets of my bed. I know what it's like to have a stark naked woman standing before me and overcome the temptation to indulge in the pleasures of the forbidden.

I also know what it's like to fall prey to the flattering lips and seductive ways of a woman. I've lost my virginity and wailed at the altar for mercy and forgiveness. I've been enslaved by the spirit of lust that has led to fornication, masturbation and pornography. I've been addicted to the feeling that has led to a physical high and resulted in a spiritual low. I've been in service and have had sin waiting for me in the church parking lot.

However, I've overcome the spirit of lust, entered into a godly relationship and successfully maintained a lifestyle of abstinence until the appointed time (marriage). There is no better joy than firmly standing on the Word of God and reaping a harvest of blessings that is exceeding abundantly above all that one could ever ask, think or even imagine. I've gone full circle and have experienced both the curses of disobedience and the blessings of obedience. So, I humbly believe that I am qualified to teach the children of God how to overcome sexual sin and stay on the path of sexual purity.

My prayer is that *PIMPIN' From The Pulpit To The Pews: Exposing & Expelling The Spirit Of Lust In The Church* will cause a spiritual revolution to take place in the church. However, this revolution will not be like those in the days of old. This revolution will cause people to preach, proclaim, and practice chastity among the singles and fidelity among the married. This revolution will break generational curses, bind the forces of hell and loose the power of heaven in the lives of God's people. This revolution will spread beyond church walls into the streets of our nation in order to reclaim the order and divine will of God. Read this book, pick up your weapon (the bible) and fight the good fight of faith.

PIMPIN' From The Pulpit To The Pews

Hallelujah!
Let the church say AMEN!
Is how the service begins.
Hands raised for praise
Eyes fixated on thighs
Loose spirits, lost souls
Men and women completely livin' out of control

There's a spirit in the house
A spirit of lust no doubt
Can somebody help me?
I need to find a way out!

My flesh exposed
My lust expelled
My spirit is falling into the pits of HELL!

Lonely days, dark nights
Callin' on PASTOR to make everything alright
I need healing hands to ease this pain
This carnal desire has become a stain
My eyes are crying, my spirit is dying,
I'm sick and tired of test-i-lying!

What should I do?
What should I say?
Oh Lord, if you hear me please make a way
This secret world I must confess
Operating under the enemy's best------HAND!
I can't withstand------the thoughts of being with another
man
Oh Lord forgive me and help me please
I'm falling down on bended knees

Misguided eyes lost in darkness
This prodigal child I have become
I'm ready now Lord let your will be done
So lead me Shepard and show me your ways
My temple was made to glorify your name
You said in your word........you'd never leave me
I'm not forsaken..... I'm seeking you now
I surrender Father please show me how
In order to survive and be set free
I must infect the TRUTH
To live eternally

Ladi Di

PIMPIN' From The Pulpit To The Pews

There's A Spirit In The House

The Power Of A Preying Preacher

he Secret Underworld Of Homosexuality In The Church

Teen Sexuality: Is There A Virgin In The House?

Overcoming The Lust Of The Eye

Help: My Body's Yearnin' And My Flesh Is Burnin'

Killing The Spirit In The House

CHAPTER 1

THERE'S A SPIRIT IN THE HOUSE

"Praise the Lord and pass the condoms!" This disturbing but candid phrase has summed up the seemingly paradoxical lifestyle of many people within the church. During the hours of Sunday morning worship millions of people throughout the nation come into the church to fellowship with other believers, receive a rhema word, enter into corporate worship and render a monetary offering unto the Lord. Unfortunately, once the benediction is given, countless churchgoers spend the remainder of the week offering their bodies as living sacrifices to the insatiable desires of their flesh. This deplorable state of affairs has become too common within the body of Christ.

When the doors of the church are open, the experiences shared among believers are like no other. It is often a spiritually charged atmosphere with continual accounts of healing, deliverance and salvation. Pastors preach and teach deep revelatory Word that well equip their members to fulfill the call that God has upon their lives. Praise teams, choirs and praise dancers work together to help usher people into the presence of the Lord. Members randomly shout, run up and down church aisles, lie prostrate, lift up holy hands and shout praises unto the Lord throughout the course of the service. When everyone dwells on one accord, all leave the service emotionally stirred and spiritually fed. Church growth remains steady and its members stay spiritually healthy.

This awesome description, however, does not describe the makeup of all churches. With well over 350,000 churches and 230 denominations within the United States, a substantial proportion of the church is struggling with the affairs of the flesh. Its very members comfortably fade into the overall landscape of the church. These are members who serve from the pulpit as well as dwell amongst the pews.

Who are they? They are the members who struggle with a legitimate weakness. They are the leaders who spiritually manipulate and wickedly prey on the naïve. They are the infrequent attendees who periodically pop up to knock up an unsuspecting soul. They are the spiritual babes who struggle with burying their sinful past. They are the sexually curious who have never encountered the experience of sex. They are the sexually repressed who are itching to once again splurge in the pleasures of ecstasy. They are the individuals who have been handpicked and assigned by Satan to seduce and slaughter the upright. They are those who have transformed the sanctuary from God's house to a whore's house.

The church has become a hotbed for the sexually indiscriminant. It has taken on the essence of a whorehouse. A whore is a person who is considered sexually promiscuous. A person considered as having compromised principles for personal gain. The church is full of people who have taken on this description.

People from every imaginable walk of life sit in church pews every Sunday. Their reasons and motives for attending church vary. Many women come to church hoping to find a husband. Countless men come to church in search of desperate and lonely women to sexually exploit. Several come to hide under the banner of religion while they continue to entertain their carnal appetites. Many are rebellious church babies who are ready to sexually make up for all the time that has been lost holding on to their virginity. Others attend because of family or cultural tradition but feel no moral obligation to abide by the creed of sexual purity. And the list goes on.

The spirit of lust has crept into the church and has brought its demonic cohorts along with it. They are as follows: The spirit of seduction, the spirit of flirtation, the spirit of adultery, the spirit of self-indulgence, the spirit of homosexuality, the spirit of lesbianism, the spirit of sodomy, the spirit of incest, the spirit of pornography, the spirit of fantasy, the spirit of masturbation, the spirit of prostitution, the spirit of addiction, the spirit of obsession, the spirit of habits, the spirit of loneliness, the spirit of inordinate affections and the spirit of idolatry.

These spirits have manipulated the teachings, beliefs and behaviors of those within the church. Many of our worship centers have become like the church in Thyatira that was full of sexual sin. God expressed his disappointment to this church in Revelations 2:20. *"Yet I have this against you: You are permitting that woman Jezebel, who calls herself a prophetess, to teach my servants that sex sin is not a serious matter, she urges them to practice immorality and to eat meat that has been sacrificed to idols. (TLB)"*

Sex has not been given the attention that it deserves within the body of Christ. For this very reason, it has been one of the most overwhelming problems in the church. A former Baptist preacher once said that sex within the church is so bad that condoms should be passed around in offering baskets and preachers should be the first in line to receive them. Dirty deacons, evil elders and perverted preachers have relentlessly sexually preyed on their own congregations.

Choirs and praise teams are full of people who sing the gospel but don't live it. They sing "Lord, prepare me to be a sanctuary, pure and holy, tried and true." Yet, they hum the tunes of sexually provocative songs while they partake in the pleasures of sexual sin. They entertain rather than minister because they're spiritually empty. They sing unto the Lord but there's no joyful noise. It's just noise. Their voices and instruments have become like sounding brass and tinkling cymbals.

Members secretly sleep with one another in the church. Husbands sleep with single and married women. Wives are guilty of the same wicked behavior. Teens sleep with other teens. Children wait until parents aren't present and experiment with one another. Older men sodomize young boys. They also prey on young girls and rob them of their virginity. Both men and women are raped by other so called 'brothers and sisters in Christ'. Babies are molested. Curious kids dabble in homosexual acts while others flaunt their lifestyle before all to see. This immoral behavior has caused many of our churches to die a slow death and something must be done.

Hotels, Motels & Holiday Inns: The Church Convention

Every year church organizations select a city to host weeklong national conventions. Church members travel by train, plane and automobile from all fifty United States to attend the 'event of the year'. Hotels are quickly sold out. Convention center parking lots are laced with church vans and chartered buses. Streets are congested with people walking to and from local restaurants and shopping centers.

Continually, throughout the day, workshops and seminars are conducted. Ordination ceremonies are held for the appointment of elders, pastors and bishops. And convention center ballrooms are crammed with fabulously dressed church folk anticipating the scheduled guest speaker for the night. Many travel hundreds of miles to receive healing, deliverance and empowerment.

Others travel the same distance to engage in uncensored sexual pleasure. Church conventions have become a fantasyland for numerous people. Many lounge in hotel lobbies, parking lots and conference hallways to meet and greet while others diligently hearken unto the voice of the Lord. Rather than lying prostrate in the presence of the Lord, many secretly dwell in hotel rooms and lie prostrate in the presence of the lustful.

It's as if many have turned church conventions into religious freakniks. There is no public display of two-piece bathing suits, video camcorders or wet t-shirt contests. However, these conventions have become a secret world of sexual free-for-alls. People of all ages vehemently indulge in the pleasures of the night even in the midday hour.

While parents go off to morning and midday sessions, pre-teens and high school-age children are left to wander the streets all day long. Once the coast is clear, huddles of kids slip into hotel rooms and indulge in carnal fiestas. Boys strip bare and randomly flash intrigued female onlookers. Sensual games such as spin the bottle and truth or dare are played. These same children separate by pairs into bathroom tubs, closets and under bed covers and fondle to the point of stimulation, while others wait in eager anticipation for their turn to come. Partners are exchanged and the process begins all over again.

College students and young adults are often more advanced in their sexual pursuits. To no surprise, most engage in full-blown sex. Often, sexual partners are familiar faces from other churches that are reunited for a week of pleasure. Others are individuals who are formally met for the first time. After a few days of verbal exchange, the stakes are raised and the interchange becomes sexual. Group sex is not an uncommon experience for young adults as well. Heathen festivals (orgies) and ménage a trois have been conducted at conventions. Some women have even allowed a group of men to systematically partake in her holy of holies.

Well, if you think that it stops there, brace yourself. You couldn't be any further from the truth. Married men and women have sunken to an all-time-low by indulging in the pleasures of others, while their spouses were not present. One married man cleared his entire day and sexually entertained four different women while his wife and family were in workshops. He secretly contacted these women days before the convention and scheduled various sex sessions in his hotel room like clockwork.

Clergy are certainly not exempt from this vile behavior. Some clergy have been known to get together and go to local nightclubs, meet girls and take them to hotels way across town and have sex with them. Some pastors and bishops even secretly have sex with each other's wives without anyone's knowledge. While they slip many of their colleagues' handshakes, they cleverly slip their wives room keys.

One year a traveling minister partook in a sexual rendezvous with another pastor's wife during a morning session. To his surprise, his wife left the workshop early to retire back to the hotel room. Once the door opened, she found her husband and the other woman in between the sheets of the hotel room's queen size bed. Without much thought, the wife lunged over her husband in a

23

rage and began to severely beat on the other woman. The incident was later brought before the board of presbyters and the evangelist was given a slap on the hand and silenced for a year.

Houston, Atlanta, New Orleans, New York City, Charlotte, Dallas, Phoenix and Philadelphia are just a few of the hotspots that churches have used to host their national conferences. While most have received information, inspiration and revelation from a week full of powerful and anointed services, several have returned home broken, abused, humiliated and possibly infected by others they may never again meet. Marriages have been broken and careers destroyed by individuals who chose to operate outside of the will of God.

Saved, Single & Unsatisfied

The church is busting at its seams with single men and women struggling to remain sexually pure. Sadly, many singles in church pews are so pre-occupied with sex that they are willing to indulge in sexual passion without regard for any consequences. Rather than embracing the season of singleness as a time to focus on and celebrate the joys and accomplishments of self, they focus on their relational status and unyielding passions and fall even deeper into the deplorable pit of desperation and loneliness.

In order to understand how serious this state of affairs truly is, you must consider the diversity of the single classification. Single is not synonymous with youth. Singles come in all ages, shapes, sizes and disguises. They range from the young teenage single parent, to the 23-year-old college student, to the 35-year-old divorcee all the way up to the elderly widow. Among this group are men and women, of all ages, raging with hormones that ultimately shape their sexual behavior, even within the walls of the church.

Center isles in the sanctuary often look more like fashion runways during offering time. Some young women walk by in tight skirts, bra-less designer tops, dips and splits, high heels and too much make-up – looking like they're headed for a club instead of church. With very few available men, some women seize every opportunity to look their best and catch the eyes of unsuspecting men. They twitch, wink and even stare to draw the attention of the men they're trying to pursue.

Dr. Wanda Davis-Turner, in her book *SEX Traps*, clearly expressed what takes place on a typical Sunday within the wall of the church:

"Women will dress provocatively to excite the fantasies of men in the church by entering God's house in scanty outfits designed to get their attention. To be specific, I have seen women prancing down the aisles with everything "hanging out." I've seen them come in with no bras, no panties, no girdles, no jockey shirts, and no T-shirts...Men can be just as bad with their tight jeans or dress slacks, and with their openly lustful glances – or stares – at every female in God's house."

Unfortunately, the ratio of single men to women in the church creates an enormous problem. Women have been known to fight over any new man who has recently come into the church. Best friends and family members have fallen out with one another in attempts to obtain a man. These women have stopped at nothing to get what they want.

The term 'desperate times call for desperate measures' is not a far-reaching philosophy for many women in the church. They have spent an incalculable amount of time fasting and praying for God to send them a man. In an unsuccessful attempt to get their prayers answered, they make a decision to step out on their own and seek married men, gay men, unsaved men, cheating men, lying men, jobless men, younger men, older men, blind men, crippled men and even crazy men. They give their bodies away in exchange for companionship and false love. They've often felt that it was the only way to get and keep a man.

Ironically, in the world, the rules have always been clear: 'men chase and women choose'. However, in the church, the inverse has been proven time and time again to be the case. "Women chase and men choose." The bible is very clear what the order of relational affairs should be. Proverbs 31:10 says, "Who can find a virtuous woman? For her price is far above rubies (KJV)." Proverbs 18:22 says, "Whoso findeth a wife findeth a good thing, and obtaineth favour of the Lord (KJV)."

It is certainly clear that the man is responsible for chasing a woman. Any woman that is known for chasing a man is completely out of order. The man, however, must be brought into question? What kind of man is he?

What are his motives and intentions? These are very legitimate questions to ask because the assumption cannot be made that all church men are good men. On the contrary, many men will bypass women in the club and in the street in order to get a 'church girl'. The reason for most men is usually two-fold. Either, they want a virgin or a freak. They believe both can be found in the church.

After men have gotten tired of the sex game, they often desire to pick from the fruit of an untouched tree. They don't mind being involved with sexually experienced women as long as it's not their wives. Meanwhile, other men seek women who are willing to try anything. These are women who are either very sexually curious or sexually experienced. The curious women usually find themselves battling with repressed erotic desires that they are willing to explore. Meanwhile, the experienced women desire to continue in their sexual pursuits.

Many single men sit in pews every Sunday hawking potential eligible women. These are men struggling with the spirit of lust. Though, they've accepted Jesus Christ as their Lord and Personal Savior, their minds haven't been renewed. Profanity, pornography and casual sexual behavior is still on their minds. They've come into a completely different world with a new set of rules. The world encourages sexual promiscuity and the Word commands sexual purity. They are now expected to give up the very thing that has motivated many of them to wake up in the morning. Sex! As a result, many carry the spirit of lust into and throughout the church by having sex with the saints of God.

The unsatisfied men in the church have been known to lay down their beliefs, fulfill their sexual appetites and pick their religion back up once the deed has been done. They masturbate, have sex with married women, single women and any other women willing to allow them to sample the sweet nectar of their secret garden.

These are the same men who get into comfortable social settings with other men and explicitly discuss every woman in the church; who looks good, who's got a bangin' body, who's available, who's a freak, who's mission impossible and who's next on their list. They run through every willing woman in the church with a barrage of empty dreams and false promises. Many of these men act like commitment-phobic "dogs" because they have the ability to pick and choose from a surplus of women in order to fulfill their sexual desires.

The men and women who secretly struggle with their flesh often run to the altar to legalize their passions. They travel out of state, secretly elope and come back married. Others privately get married by a pastor or judge in order to remove the guilt and shame from their lives and publicly wed several months or years later.

Unfortunately, others don't make it down the isle in time and wind up pregnant. In attempts to further cover up their actions, they terminate the pregnancy. Quite a few women in the church have had countless abortions in order to avoid public humiliation. They've feared the opinions of men more than the commandments of God.

Meanwhile, others keep their babies and usually bear the responsibilities alone. Typically, when the relationships go sour, either the man or woman, wind up leaving the church for good just to wind up in the same trap somewhere else.

This perpetual cycle continues to play itself out over and over because an inadequate amount of teaching is done on the sexual struggles of being a Christian single. Singles conferences and special services are often conducted by married ministers who often tell them to 'just hold on.' They are usually given unsuccessful antidotes to fix their problem. They are told to spin around, theoretically spinning right out of their situation. They are told to shake it off. In theory, they are shaking off the residue from their sinful past. They are told to take two-step forward, stepping out of a world of sexual sin. Lastly, but certainly not least, they are told to write down a bunch of names on a piece of paper, ball it up and throw it over your shoulder, thus throwing those individuals out of their lives.

Unfortunately, these quick fix solutions are generally designed to fail. There is no Word involved, just emotions and mechanical demonstrations. Even though they may be emotionally strong in the midst of a high-spirited service, once the benediction is given and there is no longer any Hammond organ to shout to, the spirit is willing but the flesh is weak. As a result, unmarried men and women in the church remain saved, single and unsatisfied.

There's A Spirit In The House

One of the biggest problems in the church is that we have eagerly embraced the fellowship, customs and cultures of the world. Rather than influencing their traditions, we have allowed their traditions to influence us. The children of Israel were notorious for allowing pagan cultures to draw them away from the true purpose and presence of God, which ultimately led to their demise. Even though we are thousands of years removed, we continue to make the same mistakes the children of Israel made.

There's a spirit in the house because we have mingled with the affairs of the world and have brought its spiritual residue back into the church. Israel never abandoned God. However, they incorporated other gods into their daily worship. Regretfully, the same gods the children of Israel worshipped thousands of years ago, we continue to worship today. In order to truly understand the alarming state that the church is in, we must go to the scripture. Numbers 25:1-3 states:

"While Israel was camped at Acacia, some of the young men began going to wild parties with the local Moabite girls. These girls also invited them to attend the sacrifices to their gods, and soon the men were not only attending the feasts, but also bowing down and worshiping the idols. Before long all Israel was joining freely in the worship of Baal, the god of Moab; and the anger of the Lord was hot against his people (TLB)."

This verse shows the great challenge Israel had to face. The most dangerous problem for Moses and Joshua was not Jericho's hostile army, but the ever-present temptation to compromise with the heathen Canaanite religions and cultures. The primary Canaanite religion of the land was Baal worship.

Baal worship originated under the rule of Nimrod in the great, godless Empire of Babylon. Since its origin Baal worship has existed in a minimum of 15 different forms throughout the world. It has spread from Babylon to Greece, Rome, India, the Middle East, Great Britain and can be traced as far as the United States.

Baal was the most popular god in Canaan, the land Israel was about to enter. Represented by a bull, the symbol of strength and fertility, he was the god of the rains and harvest. Since Baal was so popular, his name was often used as a generic title for all the local gods. The worship of the god Baal was founded upon sexual perversion and fornication. It involved ritual sex, particularly the opening or tearing of the female hymen, presumably for fertility worship. The worship of the erect male penis was also central to Baal's religious customs.

Baal could only be appeased through sex. The temples erected unto Baal were comprised of altars, which were made of beds. Men and women would worship on the altars by performing sexual acts before Baal in order to please him. This form of worship was not spiritual, rather entirely physical. It was based upon hormones, uncontrollable passions and desires. It was sensual, lustful, carnal and fleshly. It incorporated the

31

practices of pre-marital sex, extra-marital sex, oral sex, anal sex, vaginal sex, masturbation, sodomy and a host of other sexual acts.

If an individual wanted to worship Baal and hadn't a sex partner, he or she would go into the temple courts and solicit the company of a prostitute. For a small fee, the prostitute would take any willing person into worship. There were both male and female temple prostitutes. They would often perform the most vile and perverted sexual acts as a part of worship. Many often performed acts of ritual fornication publicly. Both, heterosexuality and homosexuality were practiced and encouraged as a form of worship. Men would take other men to the altar if they were gay. Women would do likewise.

All sex acts were intended to meet one purpose, the sacrificial offering of sperm from male ejaculation. The human seed was given over to Baal's demonic beings. It was believed that the god Baal would give favor and blessings of fertility, virility and harvest in exchange for ritual acts of fornication and adultery.

The whole philosophy of Baal worship was sex no matter what form it came in. Large altars and temple courts were reserved for heathen feasts. Heathen feasts were other wise known as ménage trios or sacred orgies. The people would get together, get very drunk, and engage in promiscuous sex. The stated reason for this ceremony was to celebrate and thank their gods for the success of bearing children, breeding animals and growing crops.

Another form of worship to the god Baal was the sacrifice of infant children. Ahaz, king of Judah, led his people into Baal worship along with the sacrifice of his own children in the Old Testament. Ahaz went so far as to burn his son as an offering. (2 Kings 16:3). It was believed that human sacrifice to Baal held the key to prosperity. Therefore, selfish people desiring to live in prosperity brought their firstborn child to the high priest, where the child would be offered as a burnt offering to the deity.

The altar of Baal was in the image of a bull with the head and shoulders of a man. Its arms extended outward and fire belched out from a hole in the chest. The priest of Baal placed the babies on the outstretched arms, where the child would be rolled into the fire. As the child died, the priest and priestess engaged in sexual intercourse, while an orgy occurred among the onlookers. Some accounts suggest that people would also sing religious hymns very loudly at this point to drown out the baby's screams. Since that time, archaeologists have unearthed Baal cemeteries and discovered the remains of more than twenty thousand children.

According to Malcolm Muggeridge "Sex is the ersatz or substitute religion of the twentieth century." As true as the statement may be, it is certainly not complete. Not only has sex become the substitute religion of the twentieth and twenty-first century, it's roots extend as far back as Sodom and Gomorrah. However, it has traveled all the way up into the new millennium. Today, Kama Sutra and Tantric sex are its most notable forms of practice. These Indian religious orders are deeply routed in Baal worship. But it also comes in many

33

other forms. Baal worship remnants are found in nude public beaches, pornography, magazines, homosexual clubs and bathhouses, brothels and red light districts and group sex clubs of cities worldwide, to name but a few examples.

Sadly, many Christians have allowed the spirit of Baal to enter into the body of Christ. Many have ignorantly incorporated Baal worship into their lives. We go to church once, maybe twice, a week and worship the true and living God. But, every other day of the week many of us unconsciously offer up our bodies as living sacrifices to Baal.

Each and every time you indulge in the pleasures of fornication, you are partaking in a form of demonic worship. If you are guilty of participating in extra-marital affairs, you are also guilty of entering into demonic worship. If you are a masturbator, gay, lesbian, a child molester or a proponent of pornography or prostitution, you are unknowingly but voluntarily participating in Baal worship. If you willfully terminate (abort) a pregnancy for your own personal gain, you are unconsciously offering up a sacrifice to Baal.

Not only was the worship of Baal performed, the culture of Baal was adopted. The children of Israel were guilty of embracing the heathen Canaanite culture and we continue to make the same mistake. Raw sexuality is grossly portrayed throughout every media outlet. There is a relentless portrayal of the highly sexed, large-breasted beauty and the physically well-endowed stud excessively depicted in videos, magazines, music, film and television.

Magazine publications are seemingly obsessed with exploiting and influencing its readers' sex lives. Publishers seek to seduce potential readers with sexually provocative sub-topics that glare at them from newsstand racks. Late-night television remains bombarded with phone sex advertisements. Mid-day soap operas have become visual romance novels that offer step-by-step enactments of infidelity, overbearing promiscuity, excessive greed and scores of lies and deception. Talk shows draw heavily on relationship topics centering on dysfunctional family issues, sexual activity and dating. Music videos have become short-lived light porn movies that entice one to commit sexual sin. Just about every radio station plays music that highlights materialism, false definitions of man/womanhood, fornication, infidelity, homosexuality and the elusiveness of spirituality.

Everywhere you turn, Baal and his demonic cohorts are enticing you with throes of sexual passion. Sadly, many saints within the body of Christ have jumped in headfirst. They have become soaked and saturated with the spirit of lust. The spirit of Baal has swept through the church and its damaging effects have come crashing down on the saints of God. Joshua 24:31 says, *"...choose you this day whom ye will serve; whether the gods which your fathers served that were on the other side of the flood, or the gods of the Amorites, in whose land ye dwell; but as for me and my house, we will serve the Lord (KJV)."* Whom will you serve, God or Baal? Will you serve Jehovah, the God of Abraham,

Isaac and Jacob? Or will you serve Baal, the god of the Canaanites? You can't serve two masters.

In order to get the spirit out of the house, you must make sure that the spirit is out of your house. Your body is the temple of the Holy Spirit. But, is the Holy Spirit dwelling within your temple or have you allowed the spirit of Baal to enter in? God and sin cannot occupy the same space. Therefore, a decision must first be made in you. Allow God to use your members for His righteousness, not Baal's wickedness. When this is done, victory will come to every believer within the Body of Christ.

PIMPIN' From The Pulpit To The Pews

There's A Spirit In The House

The Power Of A Preying Preacher

Secret Underworld Of Homosexuality In The Church

Teen Sexuality: Is There A Virgin In The House?

Overcoming The Lust Of The Eye

Help: My Body's Yearnin' And My Flesh Is Burnin'

Killing The Spirit In The House

CHAPTER 2

THE POWER OF A PREYING PREACHER

Jasmine, a former, devout member of a flourishing church in the south, and her 16-year old daughter have spent several years wrestling with one horrifying commonality; they were both betrayed by the same minister. Jasmine, as well as, her only child were repeatedly molested and ultimately raped at age twelve by the least likely suspect in the church: the pastor. First Peter 5:2,3 says *"Feed the flock of God, care for it willingly, not grudgingly; not for what you will get out of it, but because you are eager to serve the Lord. Don't be tyrants, but lead them by your good example (KJV)."* Countless men and women of the cloth have slept with the very flock for which they were responsible.

During Jesus' walk on the earth, He spent precious time with his disciples, Peter, James and John in particular. One day while Christ was praying on the mount, He noticed Peter's drowsiness. Swiftly, Jesus warned in Matthew 26:41, *"Watch and pray, that ye enter not into temptation: the spirit indeed is willing, but the flesh is weak (KJV)."* When Jesus told Peter to watch, He meant for them to be aware of the possibilities of temptation, to be sensitive to its subtleties, and to be spiritually equipped to fight it. Also, prayer was encouraged to acquire God's strength to help defeat Satan's power. Over the course of time, this very scripture has been severely misused and abused. Many of Christ's modern-day disciples (otherwise known as preachers) have brought shame to this unadulterated teaching.

Preachers watch and **prey**, instead of being obedient to the command to watch and pray, simply because their flesh is willing and their spirit is weak. Rather than watch to avoid temptation, they watch to embrace temptation. Much time is spent carnally watching the faces, figures and frames of unaware parishioners who freely come and go in and out of church without reservation or hesitation. These unsuspecting women are sized up from the moment they walk in until the moment they walk out. Once the carnal clergyman identifies his woman of choice, he then makes an all out effort to prey on her.

Forbidden behavior such as sexual jokes, subtle erotic innuendos, inappropriate touching, excessive compliments, flirtation and gift giving are just a few of the things that ministers have done to cross the line. Minister's ill intent coupled with a parishioner's naivety has often gotten both parties in trouble. The laying on of hands ministry has moved from the pulpit to the secluded dwellings of its parishioners. For many ministers, it's become a cheap thrill that breeds forbidden pleasure. Carnal clergymen's single objective is to prey. In other words, to hunt, devour, feed on, attack, pounce, consume, exploit and to victimize someone or make a profit at someone else's expense. Rather than watch and pray for our women, many secretly watch and prey on our women.

The Pastor's Harem

The book of First Timothy is very clear about the duty of clergy (deacons, elders and bishops) to be the husband of one wife. When the Apostle Paul declared this before the leadership of the church he was prohibiting both polygamy and promiscuity. However, many have disregarded Paul's teaching. Sexually immoral pastors, preachers and teachers continue to practice Old Testament ways in new millennium days.

Before the ministry of Christ, leaders (kings) and men of great wealth acquired harems. As recorded in the Old Testament, kings collected not only vast amounts of jewelry, but also great numbers of women. Esther 2:3 says, *"...Let us go and find the most beautiful girls in the empire and bring them to the king for his pleasure. We will appoint agents in each province to select young lovelies for the royal harem. Hegai, the eunuch in charge, will see that they are given beauty treatments, and after that, the girl who pleases you most shall be the queen instead of Vashti...(TLB)"*

These beautiful young women were slaves, foreign captives of war and virgins taken from their homes and required to live in a separate building near the palace, called a harem. Young girls were brought to the harem and given extensive training and beauty treatment before they

41

were made available to the king. Their sole purpose was to serve the king and to await his call for sexual pleasure.

Though polygamy was a socially acceptable practice for kings, God specifically warned against it. Deuteronomy 17:16,17 says, *"The king...must not take many wives, or his heart will be led astray (TLB)."* Numerous wives have eventually turned many kings away from God. Unfortunately, within many of our churches, harems are not just an Old Testament truth but a modern day reality. Harems have gradually become an exclusive amenity among immoral leadership. The church is full of women who have unsuspectingly gained the attention of their spiritual head. Lustful eyes, carnal thoughts and unquenchable appetites have influenced minister's unrelenting chase. The hunt does not cease until the desired numbers of women are obtained.

Underground harems are generally never similar with respect to the choice of women selected by a pastor. Ministry heads, personal assistants, choir members, teen and college-age girls, as well as associates of churches from across town are among the pickings of carnal clergy. Unlike harems of old, leaders of today have sexual subjects that are not aware of each other's relationship to the pastor. Remember, it's a secret.

It's a secret life of clandestine emails, undercover messages, sneaky phone calls and back room heathenism. Midnight rendezvous across town in unsuspecting sleeping quarters are not atypical for many men and women of the cloth who choose to indulge in such perversion. However, the overwhelmingly arrogant don't go to such extremes to conceal their immoral deeds. Believing somehow that they are untouchable, numerous boldly elect to get down and dirty within the private chambers of their own church.

Sadly, church offices have become a hot spot for pastor-parishioner activity. One pastor was caught having sexual intercourse with the praise team leader while the first lady was in the sanctuary leading devotional service. After being interrupted by a fellow clergy member, he nonchalantly placed his robe and collar back on, went inside the sanctuary to preach and ultimately tore the house down.

Ironically there was no remorse, shame or guilt. Why, you may ask? Well, it's quite clear. The immoral activity of this particular pastor is not out of the ordinary. He's become spiritually and emotionally callous to his own sinful actions. Many clergy members function with the same spiritual apathy. The notion that their wives are used for companionship and their countless mistresses are used for sex is an ever-increasing ideology among immoral clergy.

Interestingly, not all mistresses are malicious home-wreckers who have a personal vendetta against the ministers' wives. Rather, many are victims themselves. One parishioner admits "when my minister first approached me sexually, I was utterly dependent on him in many ways. I would have given up anything for him. What made me most vulnerable was my emotionally empty marriage. He was my counselor and mentor, someone who I thought had my best interests at heart. But, then he crossed the line and began manipulating me, setting me up for his own personal needs. Somehow the mentoring slowly turned sexual. And he offered me all kinds of opportunities in the church. He told me that having sex wasn't wrong, even though I didn't feel quite right about the whole thing. But who am I to question the authority of the minister?"

Research shows that most women who are sexually abused by clergy are initially approached because they are too insecure or too vulnerable to say no or, perhaps more important, too afraid to tell anyone about it. Often times they are in the midst of a life crisis and are especially vulnerable. When special attention from a minister turns sexual, women are often unprepared to stop it. The woman may emotionally need him to such a degree that she accepts all that comes along with her newfound dependency. Many victims say it was their absolute trust in their minister that got them into trouble because he would simply use women for sex while in his care.

During my college career, I read a piece of literature in my History class about an African tribe with a very peculiar tradition. (Unfortunately, I cannot remember the name of the tribe, but the information is definitely worth mentioning.) Whenever a guest, traveling from a distance land, would visit a married man's house, he would be given his friend's wife for sexual enjoyment as a form of hospitality. As primitive and disgusting as I thought this tradition was, I was completely appalled when I discovered that this behavior also exists within the church.

A traveling evangelist shared his experience of traveling cross-country for a three-day revival. The night of the service he was invited into the pastor's office to partake in a sexual smorgasbord. Several of the most striking women in the church were lined up in the pastor's chambers waiting to be hand picked and chosen by the evangelist for his personal delight. On another occasion, a pastor, unrelated to the first, planted a woman in the evangelist's hotel room to make his stay sexually accommodating.

These various acts of sexual immorality by clergy are detestable in the sight of God. While many struggle with sexual weakness, countless immoral clergy have chosen to live a life of sexual wickedness. God's disdain for the immoral behavior of the unrepentant clergyman or woman will result in severe punishment. Second Peter 2:1-19 clearly states:

"But there were false prophets, too...Many will follow their evil teaching that there is nothing wrong with sexual sin...These teachers in their greed will tell you anything to get hold of your money. But God condemned them long ago and their destruction is on the way...but false teachers are fools – no better than animals. They do whatever they feel like...they will be destroyed along with all the demons and powers of hell. That is the pay these teachers will have for their sin. For they live in evil pleasures day after day. They are a disgrace and a stain among you, deceiving you by living in foul sin on the side while they join your love feasts as though they were honest men. No woman can escape their sinful snare, and of adultery they never have enough. They make a game of luring unstable women...They proudly boast about their sins and conquests, and, using lust as their bait, they lure back into sin those who have just escaped from such wicked living. "You aren't saved by being good," they say, "so you might as well be bad. Do what you like, be free." But these very teachers who offer this 'freedom' from law are themselves slaves to sin and destruction. For a man is a slave to whatever controls him (TLB)."

God is serious about the salvation of His people and He will not allow those who purposely abuse and misuse their calling to be dealt with lightly. Therefore, go and sin no more.

Pastor Chasers

Though clergy have a reputation for preying on women within the congregation, many women are guilty of the same crime. Tommy Tenney, an author and minister, wrote a book entitled *God Chasers.* It was designed to help the body of Christ experience God intimately with the power of His manifest presence. However, many have shifted focus from God to the men of God, thus becoming Pastor Chasers. There are droves of sexually curious single and married women who are in hot pursuit of local preachers, pastors, bishops and traveling evangelists. These women are commonly known as church groupies. Many are lust-driven women who can't wait to get to the insides of a minister's robe. They are primarily in search of physical encounters that ultimately lead to a minister's destruction.

These women are nothing more than modern-day Delilahs. Samson was seduced by a Philistine woman named Delilah. Delilah was a deceitful woman with honey on her lips and poison in her heart. Cold and calculating, she toyed with Samson, pretending to love him while looking for personal gain. Four times Delilah took advantage of him until she ultimately brought Samson to his knees through persistent prodding, flattery and sexual suggestion. Judges 16:16-17 says, *"With such nagging she prodded him day after day until he was tired to death. So he told her everything...(NIV)."* Like Delilah, many women in the church sexual nag their minister day after day until he ultimately gives in.

Every week these women sit in church pews plotting and planning. Erotic emails, steamy lust letters, sealed with lipstick imprints, and suggestive pictures of women in tantalizing sexual positions have been but a few tactics used by these sensual bounty hunters. Provocative apparel scented with honey-dipped aromas meticulously placed alongside their sexually zealous bodies have always been their greatest scheme. They know just what to wear, how to smell, what to say and what signals to send.

Pastors are usually aware of the subtle maneuvering of women in the church, but call no attention to it because there has been no real threat. They often choose not to tell their wives, but may jokingly share it with a close friend or fellow pastor who is probably experiencing a similar scenario at his church or because of the personal enjoyment they receive from the exchange. They recognize the danger involved but continue to take the risk. Sometimes the flirting and sexual suggestion lasts for weeks, often months, sometimes longer. The longer it lingers, the more dangerous it becomes.

Altar calls are congested with women waiting in line to receive a touch. Not a touch that is holy but one that is meant to arouse. Church offices are saturated with women waiting to partake in a more intimate exchange within private counseling sessions. Some use this opportunity to express personal admirations they have for their pastor.

While others skip right through the semantics and innuendos and get strait to the point.

One woman boldly approached her pastor and said, "I'm going to have you. Oh yes. We're going to have sex and I'm going to have your baby. Not only that. You and your wife are going to break up and we are going to get married." With a stare of unbelief, the pastor looked in her eyes with disgust and told her that she was crazy.

Well, as time continued on, so did the formation of her plan. She soon discovered that Thursdays were the church secretary's day off. The coast was now clear and the plan was complete. The following week she showed up at his office in nothing but a trench coat. She had one thought, one aim and one purpose. The combination of her body, his overwhelming attraction for her and her relentless approach was too much for him to handle. From the time she arrived until the time she left her purpose was fulfilled.

This scenario is not so unfamiliar. It is very common in the church. Countless clergymen have committed adultery because they could not handle the seductive ways of sexually aggressive women. Unfortunately, once the dastardly deed has been done, the minister's life can no longer be the same. The very moment he entered into the temple of his parishioner's earthly body, a power shift took place. The degree of his vulnerability is now heightened. Now the ball is in the court of the seducer. He must return her phone calls at a moment's notice. He must make time to see her no matter how inconvenient. He must give her the attention she desires because she holds his future, ministry, finances and family is the palm of her hand. One act of incompliance of his behalf can lead to public and private humiliation and destruction.

Many women within the church make it extremely difficult for ministers to live righteous lives. Most preachers are targets of affection, especially if they are charismatic and attractive. Traveling evangelists have walked out of the pulpit to be met by attractive women who have placed notes attached with hotel room keys in their hands. Others have boldly showed up outside minister's hotel rooms completely naked. Some have even checked into minister's hotel rooms posing as their wives. One pastor responded to an emergency phone call only to be greeted, just inside the door, by a nearly nude woman with something other than pastoral care on her mind. Another pastor, while his wife and children were away, was visited unexpectedly by a seductive young woman. No tactic has ever been too demeaning for a woman on such a mission.

Ezekiel 16:31-34 says, *"You have been worse than a prostitute, so eager for sin that you have not even charged for your love! Yes, you are an adulterous wife who lives with other men instead of her own husband. Prostitutes charge for their services – men pay with many gifts. But not you, you give them gifts, bribing them to come to you! So you are different from other prostitutes. But you had to pay them, for no one wanted you.(TLB)"*

This passage of scripture clearly proves that there is nothing new under the sun. The same tactics that women have used in biblical days are ever present today. Women have attempted to get to preachers' hearts by perfecting their culinary skills. Others have bought ministers shoes, cologne, shirts, ties, suits and even more intimate apparel.

49

Hoping that he would think of her every time he adorned his body with that particular article of clothing. Ministers have naively fallen victim to allowing other women to dress them. These tactics have certainly won the hearts of many clergymen. However, the bible clearly states that anyone who would resort to such a plan to win the love of another man is worse than a prostitute.

There is another type of woman the pastor may easily get sexually involved with. Her motives aren't sinister, rather sincere. She's a member of the church, but not just any ordinary member. She has partnered up with the pastor's vision. She invests money into the ministry, intercedes in prayer on his behalf, remains involved in church committees and seeks intimacy with the Word preached on a weekly basis. She has all the vital signs of a healthy Christian except for one thing. She struggles with an intense attraction for her pastor that is accompanied by an overwhelming amount of guilt. Carnal thoughts and fantasies of love depicted through gentle expressions of intimate touch haunt her days and nights. However, it is more than some erotic form of lust, rather it is her sincere feeling of forbidden love.

Her desire for intimacy drives her behavior. She joins every committee and ministry that directly affects or involves the pastor. She's often the first to arrive and the last to leave. Wherever the pastor shows up, she strategically happens to be present. She continuously pampers the pastor with small tokens of her love. Cards, notes, prepared meals, cologne, clothes and other gestures are given to show her appreciation. These subtle gifts gradually win the pastor's heart.

Before you know it they are working closely together on various projects. Soon the pastor becomes dependent on her hard work and dedication. The more they work together the closer they become. She soon becomes his personal cheerleader and most dependable member, offering much needed support and encouragement during times of hardship. It's no surprise how this intimate relationship soon turns sexual. It is often not planned, but the intensity of the personal connection causes them both to submit to its unyielding power. Unlike the modern-day Delilah in the church, her love for him will keep her lips sealed. The secret of their sexual sin will forever remain in the bosom of her being. She will attempt to do nothing that will jeopardize his marriage or ministry.

Ministers of the Gospel, along with athletes, entertainers and politicians have been aggressively sought after by women. "But why ministers?" you ask. It's quite simple. Clergy have a degree of power because of the moral and spiritual authority of the office they hold. In addition, their education, status in the community and public image add to their appeal. It has also been said that the presence of the anointing on a minister is sexually appealing.

I have always wondered how some of the most physically unappealing ministers continue to wind up with the most striking women in the church. A preacher was quoted as saying: "When I was in the world and outside of preaching I was not popular with the girls. But, since I am now a preacher I have a new appeal and attraction." This preacher was noticeably short and chubby and from his own admission, not physically attractive. But, in his case as

51

in the case of many preachers, they found out that many women in the church just love preachers. Therefore, a preacher can look like Shabba Ranks, talk like James Brown and be as dumb as a mule and some women will love and worship him.

Interestingly, women's interests have lied more in what the minister represents than who he is. So the question remains: Would the sexual affair have happened if he was your neighbor and not a man of the cloth. Overwhelmingly, the answer is no. Many admit the clergy role carries with it a power and authority that makes attraction possible. These women feel that their pastor is the first man to take them seriously intellectually, to encourage their abilities and applaud their achievement in the church. Their faith in him compromises their moral sense.

Pastors have fallen into the arms of other women as a result of either weakness or wickedness. There are many clergymen within the church who are goodhearted, well-intentioned people who were unsuspectingly caught by the snare of women. Yet, it does not release them of their responsibility to resist sexual temptation and maintain a moral standard. Therefore, ministers must always be on guard for sex traps and continuously watch and **pray.**

Gaining So Little To Lose So Much

Adam was the first minister to walk the earth. He was personally sculpted from the hands of God and was anointed, appointed and given dominion over the entire world. He walked daily in the cool of the garden and communicated with the Most High God. Every living creature in the garden became his congregation. Adam's trial sermon was preached in the cool of the garden when he shared God's laws and commandments with Eve.

Everything seemed to be going well for Adam. He was given both favor and the provision of God, lacking nothing at all. He was given dominion over all creation. And he was even given a beautiful wife to call his own. What more could a man ask for? Adam had Money (provision of the garden), Power (dominion over every living thing) and Sex (the joy of marriage). These are three things that were entirely ordained and sanctioned by God.

But all was lost with the involvement of one act. An act of disobedience. Adam was given very strict instructions of what not to eat within the Garden of Eden. He knowingly defied God by partaking in the sweet nectar of a forbidden fruit. Though it looked good, felt good and even tasted good, it was not good for him because it was completely off limits.

What Adam gained with the knowledge of good and evil was nothing in comparison to what was lost. Adam lost dominion over the fish of the sea, the fowl of the air, and every living creature upon the earth. Adam lost a level of intimacy with Eve when he blamed her for the sin he committed. He lost his home, the Garden of Eden, and all of the unlimited provision that went along with it. Most importantly, Adam lost his fellowship with God. His divine protection, intimate communication and immediate access to God were lost. Everything was completely stripped from him because of an insatiable appetite that ultimately led to a deplorable act of disobedience.

Not only did Adam lose but all of humanity lost. The effect of Adam's sin was intergenerational. His fall led to the fall of man. One man's actions negatively affected the destiny of all human existence. Roman 5:12-14 says *"When Adam sinned, sin entered the entire human race. His sin spread death throughout all the world, so everything began to grow old and die, for all sinned. [we know that it was Adam's sin that caused this]*...(TLB)" Though we are thousands of years removed, the sin of Adam is still affecting the lives of every living creature. He will always be known as the man who had it all, lost it all and messed it up for the rest of us all.

This unfortunate scenario has been repeated time and time again by countless clergymen. A few moments of lustful pleasure have been overshadowed by hours, months, even years of shame and regret. Yet, even in the midst of shame, many are irresistibly drawn to the very thing they regret the most. This was certainly the case of one seasoned pastor.

Stricken to his knees, the pastor painfully sobbed before a fellow pastor as he hesitantly uncovered his dark secret. One morning, while drinking his customary cup of coffee, he found himself browsing through the pornographic magazine section at the newsstand on his way to work. It wasn't long before he found himself once again at the newsstand. What was once a quick browse between the covers of a Playboy Magazine, soon became a penetrable fixation on the biological makeup of print ad beauties. A few mornings later, he purchased one and days later, another.

His neurotic preoccupation with porn resulted in a rapid progression: from magazines to X-rated videos to porn theatres to the solicitation of a prostitute. But the worst was still yet to come. His act of sexual indiscretion resulted in the contraction of a sexually transmitted disease, which was quickly passed on to his wife. He was then forced to expose his hidden secret of sin so she could receive treatment. However, the damage he caused was far beyond the repair that any clinic could offer.

In the blink of an eye, all that had been established within the course of his ministry was soon lost. The 3,000-member congregation he served was stripped from under him. With no more church to lead, not only was his position taken from him, but his provision also. The comforts and accommodations that came along with being a pastor soon all dried up. The parish he gladly called home was released from him. His wife stayed with him for sometime but eventually left years later.

The shell-shocked pastor's wife suffered losses as well. The relocation they were forced to make, cost her contact with her dearest friends. Besides eventually losing her husband, she also lost her pastor. She even lost her self-worth from the act of adultery and from the ministry where she received approval. She was forced into isolation at the point of her greatest need. She was isolated and temporarily trapped in a marriage with the one who caused her all of the pain. It was hard for her to rid herself of the hurt and anger built up inside of her. Then the questions began to arise in her heart? Can I learn to trust him again?

Is it possible for me to respect him as a godly man as well as the spiritual leader of our home? These and countless other questions haunted her.

The wife's hurt affected him greatly. But when it seemed as if the world was closing in on him, matters got worse. He soon found out that his 'fall from grace' caused many within his former congregation to stumble. The sin of one man affected the lives of many. Sadly, their salvation was wrapped up in the life choices of their pastor.

This pastor's story is not an uncommon occurrence. With increasing frequency, ministers continue to fall prey to sexual temptation. When clergy choose to cross the boundaries into sexual misconduct, they must understand that they will not only destroy their own ministry but devastate many primary and secondary victims in the aftermath. In so doing, they will likely do far more harm than good, even if it is a one-time incident. However, all it takes is one-time. Adam had a one-time incident that cost him the kingdom. Many clergy have unfortunately traveled down the same path Adam has traveled. Like Adam, many have wound up with nothing. Adam and countless ministers have proven that given the right circumstances, the best among us are capable of the most unimaginable sins.

The best defense for clergy to safeguard themselves from the forbidden throes of passion is to regularly rehearse the possible consequences of sexual sin. Few people ever focus on the possible consequences of their actions. They carelessly indulge in sexual activity and deal with consequences as they arise. Such irresponsible behavior can be both spiritually and physically devastating. Complete separation from God and the risk of sexually transmitted diseases are a price that many should not be willing to pay. Every minister should continually ask himself one question. "Are a few moments of pleasure worth a lifetime of pain?" Once the question is properly answered, visually rehearse every possible consequence for such actions: disease, divorce, a broken family, a vacant pulpit, a backslidden church, dried-up financial resources, loss of home, and complete separation from God. After meditating on such a horrific outcome, pray this simple prayer:

"Dear Lord, Please Keep Me From Falling!"

Proper Discipline, Restoration & Behavior For God's Disciples

Many ministers have mishandled the call that God has given them. They've forsaken their spiritual endeavors to indulge in the pleasures of this world. I'm not referring to ministers who have fallen as a result of weakness, rather due to wickedness. These are ministers with absolutely no moral code of ethics and no true relationship with God. These are clergymen and women of the cloth who have produced no real fruit for the kingdom. If they have, their irresponsible behavior has led many astray. Unfortunately, some believers' salvation are wrapped up in the efforts of one man. When he falls, countless followers fall along with them, leaving him responsible for their souls.

John 15:1,6 says, "*I am the true vine, and my Father is the gardener. He cuts off every branch in me that bears no fruit...if anyone does not remain in me, he is like a branch that is thrown away and withers; such branches are picked up, thrown into the fire and burned (TLB)."* Immoral clergy will have their reward. Numerous clergymen have lost their churches and ministry because they've sexually mishandled people within or outside of the church.

Ministers who have been called to ministry have not gone through a transformation that suddenly exempted them from the passions, desires, and weaknesses common to all humanity. As a matter of fact, the temptations intensify as the rise in reputation and stature unfold. That is why it becomes even more important to maintain a lifestyle of sexual purity. Why? It's quite difficult to receive a word from someone in ministry who's lifestyle is too common to man (worldly). When you see a minister in the club on Saturday night sippin' on bacardi with a hottie on his arm, it's hard to then watch him deliver a prophetic message on Sunday morning.

Sunday morning pulpits are overcrowded with religious speakers and not enough spiritual leaders. Speakers are individuals who know the way and show the way. However, leaders are those who know the way, go the way, and then show the way. The missing link that seems to be prevalent is 'going the way' which simply means living the word that is proclaimed.

But, what must the church do when one of its ministers is accused of not 'going the way'? In the days of old, the accused would be brought before a court and tried. Well, what do the scriptures say regarding this matter? I Timothy 5:19-22 elaborately explains the proper procedure that should be conducted by the church:

"Listen to no accusation [presented before a judge] against an elder unless it is confirmed by the testimony of two or three witnesses. As for those who are guilty and persist in sin, rebuke and admonish them in the presence of all, so that the rest may be warned and stand in wholesome awe and fear. I solemnly charge you in the presence of God and of Christ Jesus and of the chosen angels that you guard and keep [these rules] without personal prejudice or favor, doing nothing from partiality. Do not be in a hurry in the laying on hands [giving the sanction of the church too hastily in reinstating expelled offenders or in ordination in questionable cases], nor share or participate in another man's sins; keep yourself pure (AMP)."

The instructions for discipline are pretty clear. There is an unfortunate contrast between the secret actions of the hierarchy within the Church and the stern public rebuke that the scripture calls for. Sometimes church leaders should be confronted about their behavior, and sometimes they should be rebuked (reprimanded). But all rebuking must be done fairly and lovingly, and for the purpose of restoration.

Interestingly, the minister who falls once, generally voluntarily confesses his sinful failure, and submits to a restoration process for rehabilitation. The minister trapped in a sexually immoral lifestyle rarely confesses his sin until he is exposed and typically resists any form of church discipline. Repeated fornication/adultery is more than just a sexual sin. Rather it is a mesh of issues that must be dealt with. These are issues that cannot be worked out in a brief encounter or in a three-day retreat. Neither can they be addressed while the minister is still involved in ministry. The fallen minister must be removed from active ministry in order to be restored both spiritually and occupationally.

Proper restoration should be two-fold. The issue must completely be dealt with before any consideration is made regarding being restored back into position. The primary need that should be worked through is restoration to spiritual wholeness. Fallen clergy have admitted to having a working relationship with God, rather than an intimate one. Their personal devotion have centered more around church growth and professional development than spiritual development. God requires intimacy for the benefit of the minister because he can't bear any fruit unless he continuously abides in the Father.

The minister who is serious about overcoming sexual temptation will find great help by living in the Word of God, meditating on it day and night, memorizing it and living it. His prayer will then be that of the Psalmist in Psalms 119:11: "I have hidden your word in my heart that I might not sin against you (TLB)."

After spiritual restoration has occurred, the proper role and function of church leadership should be explored. To be a church leader is a heavy responsibility because the church belongs to the living God. Church leaders should not be elected because they are popular, nor should they be allowed to push their way to the top. Instead they should be chosen by the church because of their respect for the truth, both in what they believe and in how they live. It is good to want to be a spiritual leader, but the standards are high. The Apostle Paul enumerates some of the qualifications here. Check yourself against Paul's standard of excellence. I Timothy 3:2 says, *"Now the overseer must be above reproach, the husband of one wife, temperate, self-controlled, respectable, hospitable, able to teach...(NIV)"*

The word overseer can refer to a pastor, church leader, or presiding elder. The lists of qualifications for church office show that living a blameless and pure life requires effort and self-discipline. The first requirement is for leadership to be above reproach. It means to be above shame, disgrace or blame. To live a blameless life doesn't imply to live without sin. It means to have a good reputation without stain. No leader should have the reputation of a whoremonger, a flirt or a player. His reputation should be that of an honorable man who loves the Lord and obeys His commandments.

Second, leaders must be the husband of one wife, not two or three. A leader must be the husband of one wife and not covet women that do not belong to him. He should be content with the beautiful gift of the one wife God has given him. This is where many have missed the mark. Proverbs 5:18 says, *"Let thy fountain be blessed: and rejoice with the wife of thy youth. Let her be as the loving hind and pleasant roe; let her breasts satisfy thee at all times; and be thou ravished always with her love. And why wilt thou, my son, be ravished with a strange woman, and embrace the bosom of a stranger (KJV)?"* A leader must daily seek after his wife, overcome temptation and cast all his cares upon the Lord.

Third, leaders must be self-controlled. Self-control is known as the hardest victory. It is the last of the fruit of the spirit as well as a virtue, implying that it is not merely self-effort; it is cooperating with the indwelling Spirit to make wise choices and to live in dependence on Him. People who lack self-control live by the flesh. The works of the flesh listed just before the fruit of the Spirit are sexual immorality, impurity and debauchery; idolatry and witchcraft; hatred, discord, jealousy, fits of rage, selfish ambition, dissentions, factions and envy; drunkenness, orgies, and the like. Therefore, self-control is needed in order to escape the bondage of sexual impulses. Self-control will keep one from looking with lust upon another woman. It will keep one from soliciting immoral relationships with others. It will keep one from engaging in pre/extra-marital affairs. Self-control is needed among leadership for the benefit of the entire church.

Fourth, hospitality is required among church leadership. Hospitality means to be welcoming, sociable, warm and cordial. During the early church, preaching and teaching was often done within the homes of believers. Therefore, it was necessary for leaders to be hospitable. Hospitality doesn't mean making house calls at 2:00 in the morning to a distressed saint. That's a booty call. The only thing open that late at night are a pair of legs. Hospitality doesn't mean inviting every willing female into the seclusion of church quarters for counseling. Hospitality must be met with boundaries and spiritual parameters. Too many have twisted scripture around to justify their sin. God is not pleased with such doing. Therefore, show hospitality as the scripture teaches.

Lastly, leaders must have the ability to teach the word of God. The bible warns against teaching false doctrine, myths and endless genealogies for they promote controversies rather than God's work. Teachers must adhere to sound doctrine, especially in the area of sexual immorality. Christ clearly warns the church about false doctrine in Revelations 2:14: *"And yet I have a few things against you. You tolerate some among you who do as Balaam did when he taught Balak how to ruin the people of Israel by involving them in sexual sin and encouraging them to go to idol feasts (TLB)."*

These requirements for spiritual leadership benefit both the church as well as the minister. The church leader's primary function is to love the Lord as well as those within the body of Christ. He is required to love the saints enough to effectively feed them the word of God. He must love them enough to enable people to discover and develop their God-given gifts. He must love them enough to offer training, encouragement, and a framework of support through which the ministry of all God's people can be accomplished. He must love them enough to lead them on a spiritual journey. However, it can only be done when he develops his own personal spirituality: time spent in prayer, reflection, and listening for the voice of God. He must love them enough to walk in moral integrity. When clergy know the way, go the way and effectively show the way of truth and righteousness, they successfully fulfill God's assignment.

PIMPIN' From The Pulpit To The Pews

There's A Spirit In The House

The Power Of A Preying Preacher

The Secret Underworld Of Homosexuality In The Church

Teen Sexuality: Is There A Virgin In The House?

Overcoming The Lust Of The Eye

Help: My Body's Yearnin' And My Flesh Is Burnin'

Killing The Spirit In The House

CHAPTER 3

THE SECRET UNDERWORLD OF HOMOSEXUALITY IN THE CHURCH

"NO ONE UNDERSTANDS ME, I'M SORRY!" That was my first suicide note. Those six words summed up my entire existence on earth. Twenty-six years of secrecy, lies, depression, pornography, and every form of sexual act imaginable left me wallowing in the secluded trenches of my own gut-wrenching despair. I wanted out but I kept sinking back into the quicksand of sexual sin. Every time I tried to break free from the chains of my iniquities, a demonic spirit kept pulling me back into the pit of carnality. The insufferable stench of lesbianism that emanated from the depths of my soul reeked of an eternal death.

I moved by night. I found solace in darkness for it was the only place I could hide my sin. My mind was dark. My thoughts were dark. My life was dark. The sensual give and take of every forbidden touch was exchanged with lights off, shades down and eyes closed. Even though I enjoyed the sight of the curvature frames that beheld me, I was afraid to see who I had become.

All of my life, loving women was like breathing in air. I needed them in order to survive. But after each encounter I fell into a deep despair. Being held accountable for someone else's soul was too overwhelming and agonizing for me to handle. I thought about changing my sex not to become a man but to legitimize my feelings for women. I often slept with men, both married and single, in order to live a normal life but couldn't erase the desires that yearned from within. My life was headed down a dead-end street and I soon found myself back on the roof of my building ready to jump.

In my world, homosexuality and suicide were a package deal. I found myself on the verge of suicide eighty-five percent of the time. The spirit of death took hold and grabbed me like wet denim. Two demons were constantly trying to kill me. The demon of homosexuality fought to kill me spiritually and the demon of suicide fought to kill me physically. I've attempted to jump off ledges, commit drug overdose, cock loaded pistols, drive recklessly on highways and even walk aimlessly through traffic. The only way I could kill the passions that were trapped within was to commit homo-side through the form of suicide. But I failed at everything in life, even the task of killing myself.

Fifteen lesbian relationships later, with no house, no reliable car, no college degree, no savings account, terrible credit, and no promise of any future, my love turned heartless. Every encounter became a duel, making each lover a victim in order to reclaim the power that was stolen from me in my childhood. I, through time, developed a rapist mentality. I became the man who molested me. My relationships with women were based on control rather than sexual gratification. Violence and sex became inseparable. But the pain I inflicted couldn't measure the pain that was eating me alive.

I attended church regularly with real tears and real pain hoping a miraculous change would occur. I wanted to scream HELP ME! I wanted to tell someone, anyone. But I couldn't. No one would understand. All they would do is what they've always done. Judge me. They would tell me what to do but not how to do it. I would try to enter into praise and worship but once service was over my flesh was waiting for me in the parking lot. The lifestyle trapped me and held me in bondage. But I had to break free from the bondage that has kept me emotionally scarred, physically withered and spiritually crippled.

I was sick and tired, and sick and tire of being tired. I was willing to fight even if it cost me my life. All the things that I once thought were worthwhile, I threw away in order to put all my trust and hope in Christ alone. I cut off relationships, threw away things that would remind me of my past, and stayed away from places that challenged my sexual integrity. Everything in my life became worthless when compared with the priceless gain of knowing Christ for myself. I nailed every forbidden passion and carnal desire to the cross.

Deliverance became my number one obsession. My flesh was trained to rebel and I had to break the sin cycle once and for all. I fought the memories and fantasies that took hold of my mind. I fought the feelings that consumed my heart. I fought the urges that trembled in my flesh. Throughout this yearlong ordeal, I lost a few rounds and wound up in my corner, bleeding, hurt and bruised. But my spirit often came back with an insurmountable resilience that left my flesh knocked down for the eight count.

Everyday I arose from my sleep, I geared up for whatever may have lay in my path by daily subjecting my flesh. I fought with a confidence that assured me that I am an over-comer and always triumphant in Christ Jesus. I fought knowing that I am more than a conqueror and that the fight was already won. I am now strong in areas that I was once weak. The very things that I found pleasurable now detest me. I am no longer who I once was. And I can finally testify that I have fought a good fight, stayed my course and kept the faith. Because I am free, I know that every lesbian, homosexual and bisexual can walk in freedom as well.

This testimony is one of many accounts of people within the church who have overcome the homosexual lifestyle. It may be hard. It may require a lot of discipline, but it can be done.

The Secret World Of Homosexuality In The Church

From the pulpit to the pews, homosexuals (gays, lesbians and bisexuals) have become strikingly apparent. The secret underworld of homosexuality within the church is not some pseudo-secret society that meets in remote hide-always or dark basements under dim lights. There are no initiation rituals, secret handshakes or organizational paraphernalia that can be purchased to foster gay pride and spirit. It simply doesn't exist. (At least, I don't think it does). That which used to be hidden in closets has increasingly become a very visual and integral part of the church. Homosexuals are tithe-paying members of churches all across this nation. They shout, speak in tongues, dance, and even act a fool just like any other member of a church. They're over here, over there, and just about everywhere. They're young and old, fat and skinny, dark and light, and vary in all degrees of attractiveness.

As mentioned in Black Thighs, Black Guys & Bedroom Lies, there are many who still have a very stereotypical view of homosexuals. Many envision very soft and flamboyant men with broken wrists, moist hands and relaxed or processed hair. Their mouths are contaminated with canker soars, their necks are covered with rash-like hickeys, and they speak with a high-pitched hiss, and pluralize every word. They don't just walk but they prance around in a vogue-like stride. While this image may exist, the reality is that there is no typical homosexual. Homosexuals within the church come in all shapes, sizes and disguises.

Homosexuals are ministers, deacons, and even Sunday school teachers. They are pastors who outwardly repudiate the homosexual lifestyle but clandestinely engage in homosexual rendezvous behind closed doors. They are musicians and choir members who are in committed heterosexual relationships who secretly tiptoe into the dwellings of same sex quarters. They are everywhere, hiding behind the thick cloud of masculinity and manliness. They are men who would do anything to camouflage their true identity for fear of losing their families, their jobs and their reputations.

Likewise, women are not exempt from this behavior. Lesbians are not just plain-faced, hard-core-butch types who wear short-cut naturals and boyish clothing. On the contrary, many are considered 'lipstick lesbians', very beautiful and feminine in nature. Interestingly, many lesbians attribute their overall compassion and sensitivity of women to their sexual preference. They claim to share a deep connection with one another that can never be established with men. However, sleeping with a woman doesn't guarantee anything.

The church is also bombarded with secret double agents who tip toe in and out of the beds of both men and women in order to satisfy the insatiable desires of their soul. Many married men and women are guilty of double dipping with secret sexual lovers. Sadly, many gay men and women in the church find themselves in relationships with the opposite sex, but struggle with their inner desires for the same sex. They often use the opposite sex to cover up their real identity and as a method of shirking suspicion about their sexual orientation.

There are married men, in the church, who sleep with their wives every night, yet fantasize about other men while having sex. When the opportunity presents itself, they indulge in sexual escapades with other men. What is most disturbing about this is that many who partake in the nectar of other men, don't consider themselves gay or bisexual. They psychologically block sexual labels out of their minds in order to relieve their conscience of the thoughts of guilt and shame. Many men who are married or have girlfriends, only mess around with other guys who are involved with women. One male bisexual shared his experience. "I was introduced to homosexuality by a guy I would have sex with and then he would want us to go to the club and pick up women. I was taught to not get emotionally involved."

A former lesbian in the church plainly said, "I started having relationships with men for two reasons. The first reason being normalcy. I believed God wouldn't be as angry with me if I were at least trying to do the right thing. Second, was men were my shock absorbers. Men brought me relief after women hurt me. I had sex with whatever my flesh desired for the day. The relationships never lasted long because women often left me for a man or couldn't accept the fact that I was sleeping with one. So, I sought out gay women who were in the closet and straight women in the church who were curious." Regardless of how visually noticeable gay men and women may appear in the church, this lifestyle has forced many to live their lives in a shroud of secrecy, hiding behind the shadows of obscurity.

Is There A Homosexual Theology?

There are a substantial number of gay men and women who attend church regularly and adopt the belief that homosexuality is a normal and acceptable lifestyle. They talk about God and religion with their own set of beliefs. Scriptures regarding sexual sin and homosexuality are nonchalantly overlooked or significantly challenged. Rather than accepting the truth of scripture, more time is spent trying to disprove scripture that they choose not to subscribe to. Supporters of this homosexual theology take scripture we are all familiar with, give it an entirely new interpretation, back its claims with well-credentialed scholars, and give birth to a new sexual ethic. Romans 1:24,26-27 says:

"So God let them go ahead into every sort of sex sin, and do whatever they wanted to – yes, vile and sinful things with each other's bodies. Instead of believing what they knew was the truth about God, they deliberately chose to believe lies...That is why God let go of them and let them do all these evil things, so that even their women turned against God's natural plan for them and indulged in sex sin with each other. And the men, instead of having a normal sex relationship with women, burned with lust for each other, men doing shameful things with other men and, as a result, getting paid within their own souls with the penalty they so richly deserved (TLB)."

Many who make the argument for homosexuality subscribe to the notion that David and Jonathon were homosexual lovers. *"Jonathon...how wonderful was your love for me, better than the love of women"* found in 2 Samuels 1:26 is their undeniable, irrefutable text scripture. They question how a man's love can be better than that of women unless his love with that man was also sexual. This thinking proves how misinterpretation of scripture can be dangerous. There were no homosexual proclivities between David and Jonathon. Nevertheless, lifestyle choices are based on that isolated scripture.

Genesis 1:27-28; 2:18, 23-24 is another group of scripture that is used to plead their case. The scripture states:

"So God created man in his own image, in the image of God he created him; male and female he created them. God blessed them and said to them, "Be fruitful and increase in number; fill the earth and subdue it. Rule over the fish of the sea and the birds of the air and over every living creature that moves on the ground (NIV).""

The LORD God said, "It is not good for the man to be alone. I will make a helper suitable for him (NIV)."
The man said, "This is now bone of my bones and flesh of my flesh; she shall be called 'woman,' for she was taken out of man." For this reason a man will leave his father and mother and be united to his wife, and they will become one flesh (NIV)."

The homosexual theology argues that the Genesis account does not forbid homosexuality. It simply doesn't refer to it at all. Furthermore, the scripture cannot be seen as a model for all couples: many heterosexual couples are childless, or unable to have sexual relations. Therefore, its supporters ask, "Are they in sin because they do not conform to the Genesis account?"

The theological argument is troublesome for one good reason. While it is true that the scripture doesn't mention/forbid homosexuality, it clearly provides the primary model for sexual relationships. The male-female union mentioned in Genesis is the only model of sexual behavior consistently endorsed throughout the Old and

New Testaments, whereas, every biblical account on homosexuality is mentioned in completely negative terms.

Another classic scriptural passage, used by supporters of the homosexual theology, is also found in the book of Genesis. Genesis 19:4-9 states:

"As they were preparing to retire for the night, the men of the city — yes, Sodomites, young and old from all over the city — surrounded the house and shouted to Lot, "Bring out those men to us so we can rape them." Lot stepped outside to talk to them, shutting the door behind him. "Please, fellows," he begged, "don't do such a wicked thing. Look — I have two virgin daughters, and I'll surrender them to you to do with as you wish. But leave these men alone, for they are under my protection." "Stand back," they yelled. "Who do you think you are? We let this fellow settle among us and now he tries to tell us what to do! We'll deal with you far worse than with those other men." And they lunged at Lot and began breaking down the door (TLB)."

The men of Sodom were attempting to indulge in homosexual contact with Lot's visitors. Sodom was subsequently destroyed for its great wickedness, homosexuality playing a major role in its destruction. However, many pro-gay theologians and supporters contest the notion that homosexuality had anything to do with Sodom's fall. It is thought that Lot violated Sodom's custom by entertaining guests without the permission of the city's elders, thus prompting the demand to bring the men out "so we may know them." According to the theology, the word "to know" did not necessarily have a sexual connotation. They profess that Sodom was destroyed because of the inhospitality of its citizens.

The argument makes no sense at all. Lot's response, "Don't do this wicked thing" couldn't apply to a simple request to just "get to know" his guests. Lot's second response is clear what they meant by "get to know." He answered their demands by offering his two virgin daughters. Lot's response would be senseless if the men wanted only a social knowledge of his guests. Likewise, if these men had innocent intentions, why would God have destroyed the city because of inhospitality?

Second, the theological supporters state that the real sins of Sodom, according to Ezekiel 16:49, were that it was "*arrogant, overfed and unconcerned; they did not help the poor and needy.*" These have nothing to do with homosexuality. Their argument is partially true. When Sodom was destroyed, homosexuality was a major part of its fall. Ezekiel 16:50 says, "They were haughty and did detestable things before me." The sexual nature of these detestable things is suggested in 2 Peter 2:6-7 "*If he condemned the cities of Sodom and Gomorrah by burning them to ashes, and made them an example of what is going to happen to the ungodly; and if he rescued Lot, a righteous man, who was distressed by the filthy lives of lawless men... (NIV)*" And again in Jude 7 "*In a similar way, Sodom and Gomorrah and the surrounding towns gave themselves up to sexual immorality and perversion. They serve as an example of those who suffer the punishment of eternal fire (NIV).*" As you can see, homosexuality had a lot to do with Sodom's destruction.

The last point that I want to explore is the theological premise "Jesus said nothing about homosexuality." The idea, of course, is that if Jesus did not specifically forbid a behavior, then the behavior must not have been important to Him. Stretching the point further, this argument assumes if Jesus was not concerned about something, we should not be either. So, according to the argument of silence, if Jesus did not talk about it neither should we.

The argument is misleading and illogical for several reasons. First, the argument assumes the gospels are more important than the rest of the books in the Bible. All scripture is given by the inspiration of God. The same spirit inspiring the authors of the Gospels also inspired the men who wrote the rest of the Bible. Second, it would be foolish to believe that Jesus did not care about wife beating or incest, just because he said nothing about them. There are laws against incest in the book of Leviticus. The Apostle Paul admonishes husbands to love their wives in the book of 1 Corinthians. There are many evil behaviors that Christ did not mention by name. Christ's silence on any given evil behavior doesn't give us the right to condone and freely indulge in sin. Likewise, Jesus' silence on homosexuality in no way negates the very specific prohibitions against it, which appear elsewhere, in both the Old and New Testaments.

The homosexual theological position is nothing more than an attempt to legitimize their sexual sin. Not only are there countless flaws in the their scriptural interpretation, God is not pleased with the philosophy or behavior of homosexuality. In order to overcome the lifestyle of homosexuality, it is important to renew your mind with the unadulterated Word of God.

When Homosexuality Invades The Church

There should be absolutely no ambiguity as it relates to the biblical perspective of homosexuality. The bible is very clear where it stands. Leviticus 18:22 very clearly states, *"Homosexuality is absolutely forbidden, for it is an enormous sin (TLB)."* Other translations refer to it as an abomination. An abomination is defined in the American Heritage Dictionary and the Roget's Thesaurus as vile, atrocious, deplorable and repulsive.

Several abominations, or wicked things, are listed in Leviticus 18: 1) having sexual relations with close relatives, 2) committing adultery, 3) offering children as sacrifices, 4) having sexual relations with animals and 5) having homosexual relations. It is quite interesting how these various sexual behaviors are all grouped together. They all appear to be equal in their wickedness.

These practices were common in pagan religions, and it is easy to see why God dealt harshly with those who began to follow them. Such practices lead to disease, deformity, and death. They disrupt family life and society and reveal low regard for the value of oneself and of others. Though society takes many of these practices lightly, they are still sin in God's eyes. If you consider them acceptable you are not judging by God's standards.

First Corinthians 6:9-10 states, *"Know ye not that the unrighteous shall not inherit the kingdom of God? Be not deceived: neither fornicators, nor idolaters, nor adulterers, nor effeminate (homosexuals), nor abusers of themselves with mankind, nor thieves, nor covetous, nor drunkards, nor revilers, nor extortioners, shall inherit the kingdom of God (KJV)."* During Levitical law homosexuality was punishable by death (Leviticus 20:13).

So, we can see God's disapproval of homosexuality, as well as, its punishment for such behavior. But thanks be to God for His mercy and grace. There is now redemption for all of our sins. There are several scriptures that could be listed to further explain God's disapproval for this form of sexual immorality. However, the proper response of the church is what is in question.

Typically (certainly not in all cases), the church has responded in one of two ways that have been deemed inappropriate and inadequate. Neither approach has brought healing or restoration. Both approaches have left homosexuals as well as heterosexuals completely fed up.

Many struggling homosexuals within the church feel that the church is hiding behind the bible in order to perpetrate hate and intolerance toward gays and has ultimately turned its back on its homosexual membership. Several disheartened homosexuals have even made very sharp correlations between the church and the KKK. The general consensus is that many churches judge and condemn and do little to offer restoration and deliverance apart from the "Just give yourself to Jesus and everything will be alright" cliché.

Many have spent so much time shouting the letter of the law at homosexuals, hoping to scare them into heterosexuality that they forgot to offer the love and compassion of Christ. Instead, countless ministers have dogmatically preached against every faggot, dyke, queer, sissy, butch, flamer, fruit loop, fairy, punk, switch hitter and homo from the pulpit. These cruel and insensitive words, used by many clergy, have done more harm than good. Rather than the gay and lesbian membership running to the church for healing and deliverance they have been run-off by the condemnation, repudiation and criticism of the church. Rather than people feeling comfortable enough to admit their sinful ways, they further sink into the eternal pit of silent despair. They fear confessing their faults for fear that they would be treated differently.

Church members have been known for treating gay members as lepers, handling them very delicately. They have often felt the stares of repulsed onlookers during offering time and altar calls. They have heard the self-contained chuckles of men and women during praise and worship service. They have felt the rejection and isolation on a weekly basis.

Interestingly, Christ did judge the sinner but He always gave a way of escape. Unfortunately, the church has had a problem dealing with many issues including homosexuality. Even gay support groups within churches have done a mediocre job of bringing hope and restoration to homosexuals within the church. They have taught that homosexuality is wrong. However, they've given no hope or real solutions to the problem. A woman who had been a lesbian for years went to her pastor for help and ultimately ran into a brick wall. "Well, I'll certainly pray for you," he told her. "But in 23 years of ministry, I have never known a homosexual to change for very long. I don't give you much hope." Nothing is more discouraging to those struggling with homosexuality than hearing that there is little hope for their situation. As a result, struggling gays and lesbians continue to hide in their remote sexual closets because they have received more humiliation than healing.

Generally, the second response that churches have given to the homosexual population is no response at all. Many churches have responded with a 'mums the word' modus operandi. Fear of the loss of tithe paying members has always been a concern. The loss of choir members and musicians with awesome talent has also been a major consideration. The unpardonable sin of dealing with relative topics that the church considers 'inappropriate subject matter' has also put a halt on such controversial issues. Likewise, the fear of sounding judgmental has kept such topics from being expressed from the pulpit. Pastors are sometimes confused about how to respond. They know the Bible condemns homosexual behavior, but they don't want to appear heartless.

This particular response is just as bad as the first simply because of the notion 'silence means acceptance'. Sinners, no matter what the act may be, should never feel too comfortable within the church. There should always be a pulling and tugging on every member to spiritually get it together. The comfort of one sinner will quickly lead to the comfort of another. Soon, sin will completely consume the church. There are a large number of churches that are heavily populated with homosexuals. They usher members into the sanctuary, sing in the choir, dwell among the pews and even preach from the pulpit. Not only do gays and lesbians have a strong presence in the church, the spirit of homosexuality is equally strong in the church. As a result, homosexuality is not challenged and homosexuals are not corrected.

The church has the awesome responsibility of bringing forth the gospel and ministry of Jesus Christ to the world no matter what their sexual behavior may be. The ministry of Jesus Christ was effective simply because He accomplished three things: 1) Jesus loved the people, 2) Jesus met the needs of the people and 3) Jesus taught the people.

Jesus loved lost people and enjoyed spending time with them. He was often referred to as the "friend of sinners" (Luke 7:34). Loving the unbeliever like Christ did is what many (not all) churches have failed to do. Without compassion for the sinner, our attempts to reach them will be ineffective. The commandment of love appears fifty-five times in the New Testament. So, the church's first objective is to love. Love the sinner. Love the despised. Love the rejected. Love them with acceptance. While we don't accept the sin, we should accept the sinner. Why? Love conquers all.

Second, people were drawn to the ministry of Jesus because he had the ability meet their needs – physical, emotional, spiritual, relational and financial. However, many have felt the church has failed to meet the needs of its people. The church is supposed to be about the business of meeting the needs of others in Jesus' name. Countless homosexuals are looking for answers in the church and can't find them. Their problem is ignored, overlooked or delicately dealt with. Though many churches have failed to tackle this problem, quite a number of churches are having success bringing restoration to the homosexual. Special ministries and support groups have been created specifically targeting the needs of homosexuals within the church.

Third, people were moved by the ministry of Jesus because He taught the people in practical and interesting ways. He didn't hoop and holler and tear the house down (At least I don't think He did). He didn't run around the church, tackle people to the ground and shout (dance) until he burned a hole in the bottom of His shoes just to get a message across. He taught them. The bible says that people were amazed, spellbound and profoundly impressed by His teaching. It was practical and applicable. There was no room left for doubt and confusion. He not only encouraged people to change. He shared practical steps in order for man to change. The church must also use the teaching style of Christ in order to get the best results.

If those within the body of Christ truly begin to offer loving acceptance to those struggling with homosexuality, help meet their needs and teach deliverance and restoration with practical application, change will become obtainable.

Once Gay, Always Gay, Right?

We've all heard of people being delivered from many things: drugs, alcohol, gluttony, anger, sickness and various other struggles. But, is it possible to truly be delivered from homosexuality? Do the feelings ever go away? Do the mannerisms ever change? Is the mind ever completely renewed? Is there any hope for the future? Many believe that with God all things are possible. However, others are convinced that there is no escape. Two struggling homosexuals share their testimonies:

"I myself am a homosexual, and also have a deep desire to please God, and for most of my life that has meant that I have had to deny who I was externally if not internally----because no matter what, I have never been able to shut off the attraction I have for men. I have fasted, prayed, tarried, invoked the Spirit of God to go back in time to the point of my conception and destroy the root cause of my homosexuality, prayed like Paul, believing that His grace is sufficient and His strength is made perfect in my weakness, and still my desire for men has not gone away."

Another Christian struggling with the same lifestyle earnestly shares his experience. "I have struggled with homosexual feelings and with being a born-again Christian. Now, I am married for almost 20 years to a wonderful Christian wife. My wife knows I struggle with the gay thing. I have even fallen in love with a man once, but do to marriage I couldn't honestly take the relationship anywhere."

Obviously, these two gentlemen have been overtaken by a struggle that they haven't successfully overcome. But through the power of God and the eagerness of the individual, total deliverance is attainable. The scripture bears witness for all things. First Corinthians 6:9-11 clearly says, *"Do you not know that the wicked will not inherit the kingdom of God? Do not be deceived: Neither the sexually immoral nor idolaters nor adulterers* *nor male prostitutes nor homosexual offenders nor thieves nor the greedy nor drunkards nor slanderers nor swindlers will inherit the kingdom of God. **And that is what some of you were.** But you were washed, you were sanctified, you were justified in the name of the Lord Jesus Christ and by the Spirit of our God (NIV)."*

What a great hope we have in Jesus. Those that sin in these ways can have their lives changed by Christ. Paul emphasizes God's action in making believers new people. The three aspects of God's work are all part of our salvation: our sins were washed away, we were set apart for special use (sanctified), and we were pronounced not guilty (justified) for our sins. So, the power to be freed from the shackles of homosexual bondage does exist.

Many former homosexuals have been completely delivered from the desire for same-sex relationships, while others battle with an endless temptation to sin. Fortunately, I Corinthians 10:13 assures us that temptation is not sin: *"But remember this – the wrong desires that come into your life aren't anything new and different. Many others have faced exactly the same problems before you. And no temptation is irresistible. You can trust God to keep the temptation from becoming so strong that you can't stand up against it, for he has promised this and will do what he says. He will show you how to escape temptation's power so that you can bear up patiently against it (TLB)."*

There is a difference between experiencing a pull towards homosexual acts, and giving in to that pull. We can't fully control that which tempts us, but we can choose whether or not to pursue the temptation. This power of choice is strengthened by the Holy Spirit. It is a choice to walk in sexual integrity.

Sexual integrity is an act of the will, expressed through day-to-day decisions. It's just that simple. It is a consistent lifestyle of behavior in which your sexual expressions line up with God's standards. After repentance from homosexual sin, there is usually a period of joy, freedom and newfound optimism. However, for many, it's a temporary stage that soon fades away once sexual temptation emerges. Therefore, the ability to operate in sexual integrity will keep you safe from a perpetual lifestyle of sin. Drawing clear boundaries and sticking to them is a part of the day-to-day decision making process that goes along with sexual integrity – the decision not to do what you feel the most compelled to do at any given time. Successfully walking in sexual integrity for a considerable amount of time can even lead to total deliverance of the temptation.

Interestingly, the medical profession can attest to the restoration and transformation of homosexuals. Dr. Edmund Bergler, member of the University of Vienna's Medical School, says "In nearly thirty years, I have successfully concluded analyses of one hundred homosexuals...and have seen nearly five hundred cases in consultation. On the basis of the experience thus gathered, I make the positive statement that homosexuality has an excellent prognosis (the likelihood of recovery) in psychiatric-psychoanalytic treatment of one to two year's duration, with a minimum of three appointments each week – provided the patient really wishes to change."

Dr. Irving Bieber, president of the American Academy of Psychoanalysts, says "In our judgment a heterosexual shift is a possibility for all homosexuals who are strongly motivated to change. We have followed some patients for as long as 20 years who have remained exclusively heterosexual." The testimonies of specialized doctors and physicians are endless. Not only has the medical industry experienced enormous amounts of success through clinical treatment, the church has proven to be extremely effective as well.

A great number of men have changed their sexual orientation from exclusive and active homosexuality to exclusive heterosexuality through participation in church fellowships. Many churches offer a crisis service for homosexuals, which give men and women the help they need. These support groups help people gain insight into the root causes that result in homosexuality, incest, sexual addiction and other areas of sexual brokenness. In additional, participants receive biblical help, hope and healing toward recovery. The following is a partial list of support groups within the Body of Christ that can be utilized for assistance:

Broken Yoke Ministries	www.jefnet.com/brokenyoke/
Choices	www.choices.base.org
Corduroy Stone	www.msu.edu/~cstone/
Courage	www.couragerc.net/
Cross Ministry	www.crossministry.org
Day Seven Ministries	www.dayseven.net
Deliver Ministries	http://members.aol.com/delivermin/index.html
Desert Stream	www.desertstream.org
Eagle Wings Ministries	www.ewm.org
First Stone Ministries	www.firststone.org
HA Fellowship Services	http://members.aol.com/hawebpage/

His Way Out Ministries	www.hiswayout.com
Hope Ministries	http://renewinghope.homestead.com
Imagine That Ministries	www.imaginethatministries.org/
Isaiah 56 Ministries	www.isaiah.org
Love In Action	www.loveinaction.org
Living Hope Action	www.livehope.org
Mastering Life Ministries	www.masteringlife.org
NARTH	www.narth.com
New Hope Ministries	www.newhope123.org
PFOX	www.pfox.org
The Portland Fellowship	www.portlandfellowship.com
Prodigal Ministries	http://w3.goodnews.net/~prodigal/
Recovery House	www.exodusnorthamerica.org
Renew	http://whole-man.org
Safe Passage	www.pacificnet.net/~sonia/sp.html
Transformed Image	www.transformedimage.com
Where Grace Abounds	www.wheregraceabounds.org

The notion that homosexuals have no hope for restoration is completely erroneous. God promises in His word that He is able to do exceeding abundantly, more than we can ask or think. Therefore, freedom from homosexuality is attainable for all who call upon the name of the Lord.

PIMPIN' From The Pulpit To The Pews

There's A Spirit In The House

The Power Of A Preying Preacher

he Secret Underworld Of Homosexuality In The Church

Teen Sexuality: Is There A Virgin In The House?

Overcoming The Lust Of The Eye

Help: My Body's Yearnin' And My Flesh Is Burnin'

Killing The Spirit In The House

CHAPTER 4

TEEN SEXUALITY: IS THERE A VIRGIN IN THE HOUSE?

Sex has become rampant in the church, especially amongst adolescents and teens. Teens and sex make a volatile mix as youthful passion produces curiosity and experimentation. Many of the so-called "good church kids" who go to church every Sunday and lift up holy hands unto the Lord, sin throughout the week without cause or conscience. The very ones sheltered from worldly influences, raised under biblical teaching and principles, live perverse lives of sexual sin.

By the age of thirteen, eighty-three percent of "churched" teens had experienced sexual intercourse and sixty-five percent of the youth had engaged in fondling breasts and/or sexual intercourse. According to Choosing Virginity in Newsweek, December 9, 2002, "Black students are 40% more likely to have had sex than whites."

Much of the perversion practiced by church teens is regarded as acceptable behavior. Many youth who have grown up in the church have no moral conviction about premarital sex. Several virgin Christians refuse to attend certain youth groups because they feel that the Christians who attend have far less morals than nonbelievers who do not attend. These are youth groups within Full Gospel, Pentecostal and charismatic churches. The worldly customs that are practiced by youth are not taught within the church or the home but shared in the school systems that young people attend every day. While public schools perpetuate such thinking through sex education courses, the crisis exists both in private and Christian schools as well.

Students in Christian schools regard oral sex as "Christian sex" because no genital intercourse is involved. Many have casual sex among friends and consider nothing wrong with it. Christian colleges and universities aren't exempt from such behavior. A noted Christian College had an alarming rise in sexual activity on campus. Within one school year, six girls got pregnant by young men who were studying to be pastors. These accounts are truly a crisis within the church. In order to break this cycle, proper attention and teaching must be given to youth to help them preserve their virginity.

"School's Out! What Do We Do Now?"

Buzzzzzzzz! The last school bell has finally wrung. Though it is the end of the school day, for many, the day has just begun. With no principals, teachers, parents or chaperones anywhere in sight, the sky is the limit. The combination of raging hormones, an erotic curiosity and creative experimentation, leave many students busy with extra-curricular activities.

According to the 2002 children's defense fund survey, 7 million school-age children are left alone after school without supervision. As a result students go buck wild.

Some spend countless hours searching for online porn sites. Others, as young as the sixth grade, offer sex as casually as they would a good-night kiss. Countless youth who haven't engaged in sexual intercourse as of yet, splurge in the pleasures of oral sex.

A pre-teen on Oprah said, "I do worry about AIDS. Actually, the anxiety never leaves me. But I still have sex. And I know I can always get oral sex without getting too emotionally involved." When oral sex has become too routine, teens have admitted to getting their salad tossed (oral-anal sex). Girls, and boys alike, indulge in sex purely for self-gratification.

Interestingly, more than half of our American women lost their virginity before they blew out the candle of their seventeenth birthday, and eight percent of them have slept with more than 50 guys. Not only are these kids extremely promiscuous, they also practice serial monogamy (multiple sexual relationships). Perhaps, a new partner a year. If youth start having sex at 15, by the time they are 24, in terms of the partners of partners, they've been exposed to over 500 people.

But when and where is all of this taking place? A study published in the December 2002 issue of *Pediatrics*, the peer-reviewed scientific journal of the American Academy of Pediatrics (AAP), titled "When and Where Do

Youths Have Sex? The Potential Role of Adult Supervision" looked at more than 2,000 high school students, comparing after-school supervision with sexual activity. Here's what the study found:

- Among the respondents who had had intercourse, 91 percent had last done so in a home setting.
- Fifty-six percent had had intercourse on a weekday.
- Youths who were unsupervised for 30 or more hours per week were more likely to be sexually active compared with those who were left alone for five hours a week or less.
- Those left unsupervised for more than five hours per week had more sexually transmitted diseases, particularly the boys.

What is more alarming is when the sexual activity takes place. The answers may surprise you. New data from a national survey of teens indicate that most report that their "first time" occurred in their own home or their partner's family home during the night or evening hours - places and times when many parents are likely to be around. Forty-two percent of teens reported that their first sexual encounter occurred between 10 p.m. and 7 a.m. Another 28 percent reported first having sex between 6 p.m. and 10 p.m. More than half of all sexually experienced teens reported that their first sexual encounter occurred in their family's home (22 percent) or their partner's family home (34 percent).

Beyond in-house sexual rendezvous, students explore their sexuality in many other settings. School bathrooms, classrooms and hallways have become a hotspot for greedy minors whose hormones are pulsating through their clothes. A 12-year-old girl was observed by the entire science class, performing oral sex on a classmate while an unaware teacher was present.

Another high school teacher strolled into her classroom to find a girl having sex with two boys. School buses are even notorious for sexual activity. Oral sex and unprotected intercourse have become commonplace from the time of pick-up to drop-off. Likewise, a group of students were caught having a threesome in an empty subway conductor's car near school grounds.

School parties are nothing more than a teasing appetizer for anticipated sex. Grinding, 'freakin' and booty dancing take center stage when music begins to play. Intense body contact, swinging pelvises and butts jammed up against thrusting groins peak sexual curiosity in all participants, as well as onlookers. Girls bend over, wearing thongs with their butts exposed under tight dresses, while randomly being grabbed and 'freaked' from behind by lust-driven boys. These postures are nothing more than imitation sex acts performed to a beat. After school-endorsed recreational foreplay comes to an end, evenings are typically brought to a climax with pre-arranged sexual intercourse. The prom is no different. On prom night, students participate in very adult-like behavior. The guys are in tuxedos, they've rented limos, and the girls are dressed up. Often this adult behavior includes sex.

If these incidences seem isolated or too farfetched, consider the national statistics on teenage sexuality. Though somewhat dated, the 1994 "The State of American's Children Yearbook and the 1995 State

Department of Education surveyed high school students from 58 randomly selected high schools. These were some of their alarming findings:

- Every 10 seconds a teenager becomes sexually active for the first time.
- 55% of students surveyed had sexual intercourse with another student during their high school years.
- 11% had sexual intercourse with another student before the age of 13.
- 21% had 4 or more sexual partners in their high school years.
- 46% of those surveyed used no form of contraception.
- Every 26 seconds a baby is born to an unmarried mother.
- Every 30 seconds a baby is born into poverty.
- In a 24-hour time period 2,795 teenage girls will become pregnant.
- Every day 7,742 teens become sexually active.
- 1,106 teenagers have abortions every day.

Our youth are in a state of crisis. And as each day goes by, the sex lives of our children get progressively worse. God intended for all children to have fun and enjoy their youth. However, He placed boundaries and limitations on the extent of fun to be allowed. Ecclesiastes 11:9-10 says, "*Rejoice, O young man, in your adolescence, and let your heart cheer you in the days of your [full-grown] youth. And walk in the ways of your heart and in the sight of your eyes, but know that for all these things God will bring you into judgment. Therefore, remove [the lust that end in] sorrow and vexation from your heart and mind and put away evil from your body...(KJV)"*

Teens often feel that the behavior they conduct have no affect on the future. On the contrary, many of the choices made by youth will be irreversible – they will stay with them for a lifetime. So, the message to all youth is 'Enjoy life now, but don't do anything physically, morally, or spiritually that will prevent you from enjoying life when you are old'. Sex is for an appointed time. Until that time comes, enjoy the innocence of your youth.

Rejecting Satan's Five Fold Ministry

The bible clearly expresses the significance of the five-fold ministry. Ephesians 4:11 says, *"And he gave some, apostles; and some, prophets; and some, evangelists; and some, pastors and teachers; For the perfecting of the saints, for the work of the ministry, for the edifying of the body of Christ: Till we all come in the unity of the faith, and of the knowledge of the Son of God, unto a perfect man, unto the measure of the stature of the fullness of Christ."*

The full restoration of the fivefold ministry is an important part of what Jesus is doing to build His church today. Each gift given by God has its own function and purpose within the body of Christ. God's Word reveals that the church is made up of every believer in Jesus Christ, His body joined and working together, each one doing his or her part in forcibly advancing the kingdom of God on this earth. Well, everything God creates for His people, the devil perverts. Satan also has a five-fold ministry for the perverting of the saints. The tool he uses to destroy the lives of believers, particularly youth, is the media.

Satan's five-fold ministry is exercised through the manipulation of the following media outlets: television, radio, film, print media and the Internet. These outlets are not bad within themselves. However, Satan cleverly uses these outlets for the purpose of destroying the lives of God's people, particularly our youth. The media plays a significant role in the sexual activity of young people. It successfully tells teens its okay to have sex whenever, however or with whomever they want. Surprisingly, teens rank the media as the leading source of information regarding sex. Unfortunately, these messages contain unrealistic, inaccurate, and misleading information that young people accept as fact.

A recent study found that children spend more than 38 hours a week using media (television, videos, music, computers, and video games). These adolescents view television for an average of nearly 17 hours a week and listen to music for several hours per day. On average, children between 9-17 years old use the Internet 4 days a week and spend 2 hours online at a time. By the time adolescents graduate from high school, they will have spent 15,000 hours watching television, compared with 12,000 hours spent in the classroom.

These various media sources convey one main theme: lust. Satan has used pornography as his vehicle to convey the message of lust. Pornography is any written or visual material that depicts nudity and/or sexually explicit activity for the purpose of sexual arousal. Satan uses television, magazine and radio sources to clandestinely unleash the snare of soft-porn. Soft-porn generally features scantily clothed men and women, highlighting breasts and genitalia but shows no bare sexual intercourse. Likewise, Satan uses film, print media and the Internet to blatantly unleash the snare of hardcore-porn. Hard-core pornography includes various forms of sexual positions and penetration, forced and unforced, between two or more people. Each media source has its own sexual appeal that the devil uses to lure people in.

TELEVISION

More than two-thirds of all shows on television regularly have sexual content incorporated into each episode. Sexual content include sex talk, characters planning to have sex and scenes with sexual intercourse. It has been reported that youth witness more than 15,000 sexual jokes, innuendoes and other references on television a year. Few, if any, deal with self-control, birth control, abstinence, and risk of STD's, pregnancy and HIV. In addition, according to Roger's Silent War, over 20,000 commercials annually viewed by youth send across the implicit message" "Sex is fun, sex is sexy and everyone out there is having sex but you."

Soap operas such as *The Young and The Restless, As The World Turns, General Hospital, and Days Of Our Lives* are like visual romance novels. Teens religiously tune in to watch these surrealistic television series that depict step-by-step enactments of infidelity, overbearing promiscuity, excessive greed, and scores of lies and deception. A study of 50 hours of daytime dramas found

156 acts of sexual intercourse with only 5 references to contraception or safe sex. For many, they have become the how-to of relationship immorality.

Talk shows draw heavily on relationship topics centering on family issues, sexual activities and dating. This type of content is abundant during morning and daytime hours when children have the greatest access to television. Talk show hosts such as Ricki Lake, Jenny Jones, Montel Williams, Jerry Springer and Sally Jesse Raphael have all covered very rancid topics. These topics have included dating, physical appearance, sexual activity, sexual infidelity and sexual orientation. Episode guests have included: a mother who ran off with her daughter's fiancée; a man who appeared on stage with roses for the daughter he had sexually molested, and revealed that he had been molested when he was five; a 16 year-old (wearing sunglasses to disguise her identity) who said she buried her newborn baby alive in her backyard; a pregnant woman who boasted of having eight sexual partners during her first two trimesters; and women who marry their rapists.

Music television stations such as BET, MTV and VHI relentlessly play videos that depict highly sexed, large breasted beauties and financially and physically endowed studs. The visual esthetics of these videos portray women as nothing more than eye candy. Hundreds of scantly dressed girls provocatively dance in front of a camera, licking lips and shaking hips. Videos are filled with toned legs, flawless skin, extra-long weaves and curvy hips. The videos rely heavily on breasts, behinds and crotch shots. Especially troubling is the unavoidable message that says shaking their half-naked bodies in front of a man maybe the only way to secure affection from a man.

Reality Shows such as The Real World, Ship Mates and Bachelor are very sexual in nature. For instance, Temptation Island portrays unscripted dramatic series in which unmarried couples travel to exotic locations to test and explore the strength of their relationships. Once at the location, the couples are introduced to eligible singles and then separated from their partners until the final day of their stay. Fornication, infidelity, promiscuity, and group sex is depicted as well as endorsed on reality shows.

Greg Lewis, author of the book *Telegarbage,* reported that references to intercourse on television, whether verbally insinuated or contextually implied, occurred between unmarried partners five times as often as married couples. With such a daily intake, it's no surprise that young people embrace lust over love, immediate gratification over commitment and promiscuity over celibacy.

RADIO

Most of the music selectively played on the radio highlights what is wrong with our relationships today: materialism, false definitions of man/womanhood, fornication, infidelity, homosexuality, and certainly the elusiveness of spirituality.

Flip through an urban radio station and you'll hear the same ten to twelve songs all day long. By the time you recognize the song, you've heard talk of five sex acts, a gang rape and a killing of a girl who gets out of line. "What else can you rap about but money, sex, murder or pimpin?"

says Queens, N.Y. –based Ja Rule. "There isn't a whole lot else going on in our world."

Beyond the raunchy sexual lyrics expressed in songs, many young people are more drawn by the beat and the hook in the song. Anyone in the music industry would attest to the fact that hooks (the chorus) sell songs. The lyrical content can either be irrelevant or totally misunderstood. However, the hook that is repeated over and over again throughout the song has got to grab the attention of the listener. The following hooks can be heard on the radio at any given time during the day or night.

"It's get'n hot in here,
So take off all your clothes.
I am get'n so hot,
I wanna take my clothes off. "
Nelly

"Getcha' freak on
Getcha' freak on
Getcha' freak on
Getcha' freak on"
Missy Eliot

"All I need in this life of sin is me and my girlfriend,
Down to ride to the very end is me and my boyfriend,"
Jay Z featuring Beyonce

"I just wanna rock you all night long, ooooooh.
I just wanna rock you all night long, ooooooh."

Eve

"I got my money right
Legs wide
Front back,
Side to side
Eat me right
Slip and slide
Yup, everything's gonna be alright."

Trina featuring Ludicris

Christian youth have spent more time listening to the messages of Jay Z than J.C. (Jesus Christ). They know more about Eve from the streets of Philly, than Eve from the Garden of Eden. Their ministers of music cannot be found within the four walls of a church. Instead, they are found on television video programs and in large concert halls. This degenerate hip-hop message has seeped into the souls of both Black young adults and children, stripping them of their moral core.

FILMS

The film industry has become a lot more liberal with its depiction of sexually suggestive material over the years. Soft and hardcore-porn have become common on the big screen regardless of the film's rating. Studies of adolescents have found that heavy film and television viewing has lead to the early initiation of sexual intercourse. Three out of four teens say watching movies makes having sex seem very common and normal. They have also admitted to having gotten ideas for how to talk to their boyfriends and girlfriends about sexual issues from movies.

Interestingly, only six percent of the sexual activities displayed by the media (t.v., books and movies) are between married couples. And in a research project by John Mark Dempsey and Tom Reichert, they found that 85% of sex in movies is between unmarried couples. The messages being conveyed are that sex in marriage is boring. The only exciting sex is between unmarried couples. No one is proclaiming the truth to teens that living together before marriage will severely harm them; that they will experience more sexual problems, not less; and that their odds of divorce will be 50% higher than couples who remain pure until marriage.

Dr. Gina M. Wingood of Emory University in Atlanta, Georgia conducted a study on 522 girls between the ages of fourteen and eighteen. Dr. Wingood discovered that 30% said they had seen an X-rated movie in the past 3 months. This study shows how accessible X-rated films are to youth, despite age restrictions. But what is more concerning than the number of teens viewing such movies was the real-life sexual behavior linked to it.

Wingood's team found that girls who had seen X-rated movies were more likely to have multiple sex partners as well as sex more often. Most important, the researchers noted, these girls were 70% more likely to be infected with the sexually transmitted diseases. This study simple proves that teenagers are more vulnerable than adults to having their sexual attitudes shaped by the media. They model what they see on screen, disregarding the consequences of the actions they take.

PRINT MEDIA

The advertising industry is using the exploitation of the body more blatantly than ever before. Various magazine covers feature models that are displayed and clothed in a potentially pornographic manner that successfully draw readers in. Intimate physical details are no longer being airbrushed out of photographed models; such details are even being drawn in on newsprint ad models. Many men report using these same pictures in order to fulfill their sexual fantasies while masturbating.

Most news stands stack magazines that are full of erotic content. Publications like Cosmopolitan, Vogue, The Source, Vibe, XXL, Sister To Sister and several others are seemingly obsessed with exploiting and influencing the reader's sex lives. Publishers seek to seduce potential readers with sexually provocative sub-topics that glare at them from newsstand racks.

These hook-line and sinker article topics include: Sex Bliss Secrets – Our 28 day plan that will blow his mind; Are your orgasms as amazing as they could be? 11 questions; His Body – what the size and shape reveal about his lovemaking; Is it love or lust?; What men love about your body; and The 8 things men wish we'd do more of in bed. With literary sexual themes reverberated in one issue after another, it is no wonder that this nation possesses such a gluttonous appetite for sex.

Billboard advertising and other print ads also contain a significant amount of sexual imagery, including the inappropriate use of children in provocative poses. Sex is used to sell most common products from shampoo to hotel rooms, yet when children and adolescents respond to the clues and become sexually active too young, society seems to blame young people, not the advertisers.

INTERNET

Sex is the #1 searched word on the world-wide-web and the Internet has done a great deal to sexually pollute the minds of youth. The Internet offers unparalleled access to hard-core pornography with just a few keystrokes. One recent study found that a child exploring the Internet may become trapped in an adult site by a new marketing technique that disables options such as the "back," "exit," or "close" navigation buttons. Several porn sites use popular brand names and children's characters in search engines magnets and links such as Disney, Nintendo, and Barbie, Pokemon, My Little Pony & Action Man. When these key words are used, thousands of links to hardcore-porn sites appear.

Countless pre-teens and teenagers have accidentally stumbled onto porn sites unintentionally. However, many teens have taken complete advantage of its easy access. According to *Cyberspace For Teens*, an online website, ninety percent of all kids ages 8-16 have intentionally viewed porn when using the Internet to do homework. Of the twenty-five million Americans who visit cyber sex cites between 1-10 hours a week, students are most at risk for cyber-sex compulsion. Some young adults have spent up to 10 hours at a time on the Internet. For some the Internet has become the crack cocaine of sex addiction.

Whichever media outlet grabs your attention the most, Satan's objective is to bait you with the appearance of evil and draw you into a life of sin. Reject Satan's five-fold ministry. It is designed to pervert you and put you into hell. When using the television, radio, film, print-ad or the Internet, operate with spiritual discernment and don't fall for the tricks of the enemy. Allow God's fivefold ministry (apostles, prophets, evangelists, pastors and teachers) to perfect you and bring you into glory.

As We Lay

One moment of pleasure can bring a lifetime of pain. This is a pain that is often unceasing. It can possibly be an irreversible and irrevocable pain that lasts till the very last day. Job 20:11 says, "His bones are full of the sin of his youth, which shall lie down with him in the dust." Though, this statement didn't apply to Job, it reflects the lives of millions of youth across the nation. Kelly Price said it best in the song *As We Lay*.

As we lay
We forgot about tomorrow...
As we lay
Didn't think about
The price we'd have to pay...
We should have counted up the cost
But instead we got lost
In the second, in the minute

In the hour...
As we lay
We forgot about tomorrow
As we lay
Oh no, oh no, no
My love why can't you see
How loving you is killing me...
Kelly Price

SEXUALLY TRANSMITTED DISEASES

What is the price that would have to be paid? What did they forget about tomorrow? What was it about their love that was killing? In the context of this topic, sexually transmitted disease, pregnancy, abortion and psychological distress were the outcome of such a physically exhilarating event. Some time ago there were just five major STDs that anyone had to really worry about. Now according to the Center for Disease Control (CDC), there are over 50 organisms and syndromes that are recognized as being sexually transmitted. The diseases and viruses with funny sounding names that you heard about in sex-ed class are still here, and they're growing steadily.

Today, the United States has the highest Sexually Transmitted Disease (STDs) rates of any country in the industrialized world. The CDC and Prevention, in their report Tracking the Hidden Epidemics 2000, states most people who acquire STDs in the U.S. are under the age of 25 with teen females especially being more susceptible because their bodies are still immature. In fact, a total of 3.8 million STDs are contracted each year by American teens. This breaks down to 10,000 teens per day or one every 8 seconds.

Many of those who developed AIDS in their twenties were infected as teenagers. The first stage of the deadly virus lasts ten years on average and there are no visible signs or symptoms. Therefore, it isn't possible to tell if someone is infected without an HIV blood test. Once the virus matures, half of all victims die within 2-3 years after developing AIDS and 80% die within 4-5 years.

Human Papilloma Virus (hpv), another sexually transmitted disease, causes genital warts which often reoccur after removal. The disease can cause cervical cancer among women of which teen girls who are promiscuous are 800% more at risk. Sexually active teens also have the highest gonorrhea and chlamydia rates of infection among all ages. What's important to realize is that youth can have more than one sexually transmitted disease at a time which makes their risky behavior more detrimental.

What too many young people haven't realized is that no form of birth control protects them from sexually transmitted diseases. That's why they are called birth control, not disease control. According to my previous book, *Black Thighs, Black Guys & Bedroom Lies:*

"Condoms cannot stop sexually transmitted diseases that spread from outside contact such as syphilis, herpes and crabs to name a few. The HIV virus itself is 450 times smaller than a sperm cell, about one-fifth the size of the holes in latex – the material from which the best condoms are made. So, these super small viruses can get through a hole in a condom much more easily than sperm can. The transmission of HIV can be compared to a ping-pong ball going through a basketball hoop. It's just that easy."

The small print on a box of condoms state that it helps to reduce the risk of STDs. However, there is no indication of what that percentage is. If it was successful in reducing the transmission of STDs by 1%, the statement would be true. Simply put, there are absolutely no certainties concerning the connection between condoms and STD prevention. Besides, condoms have a significant failure rate against pregnancies for those depending on them the most: young people.

According to a study done by Jones and Forrest, unmarried minorities have a 36.3% failure rate and for unmarried Hispanics, the failure rate is as high as 44.5 percent. The Alan Guttmacher Institute even reported that 43% of all unintended pregnancies occurred while using contraception. So, if they do an incredibly poor job in protecting you from pregnancy, why would you expect this failed product to protect you from a sexually transmitted disease?

The following testimony is a story of pain taken from *Tips on Encouraging Sexual Purity*. His pain is physical and hers is emotional. Both are incurable. And yet, both were preventable. Had she chosen to abstain until marriage, as he did, they could have enjoyed a lifetime of sexual intimacy without the regrets of premarital sex.

"I was married at the age of 31. My husband, a physician, was 27. He gave me the gift of his virginity the night we were married. My gift to him was herpes. Soon after our honeymoon he broke out with sores on his penis. He suspected it was herpes and later had it confirmed. Sadly, he broke the news to me. I was devastated. You see, I had no idea I had herpes. Although I am a carrier of the disease I have never had any symptoms. I gave birth to our children with no side effects to them. I consider this a miracle indeed. I don't know of a greater wedding gift a person can give their spouse than the gift of their virginity. Unfortunately, before I met my husband I lived a very promiscuous lifestyle and was unable to give this great gift to him. I have reaped what I have sown in many ways, not just physically, but spiritually, emotionally and psychologically. We have now been married many years, and when my husband suffers the physical discomfort, he rarely mentions it to me, but I know. Sadly, the love of my life still bears the consequences of my wrong doing."

The story proves that the sexual sins that you commit today can have a devastating affect on your future.

TEENAGE PREGNANCY

Unplanned pregnancy is another negative result of pre-marital sex. Almost 1 million teenagers become pregnant each year. About one out of four teenage mothers go on to have a second baby within two years after the birth of their first baby. Twenty percent of young women who become sexually active become pregnant within the first month of sexual activity. Fifty percent become pregnant within the first six months.

Among the high rate of births are serious health complications. A teenaged mother is at greater risk than women over the age of 20 for pregnancy complications such as premature labor, anemia and high blood pressure. These risks are even greater for teens who are under 15 years of age. Teens too often have poor eating habits, neglect to take a daily multivitamin, and may smoke, drink alcohol and take drugs, increasing the risk that their babies will be born with health problems.

Low-birth weight babies may have organs that are not fully developed. This can lead to lung problems such as respiratory distress syndrome, or bleeding in the brain, vision loss and serious intestinal problems. These babies are more than 20 times as likely to die in their first year of life than normal-weight babies.

A major lifestyle change also goes along with teen pregnancy. Teen mothers are more likely to drop out of high school than girls who delay childbearing. A recent study showed that only about 64 percent of teen mothers graduated from high school or earned a general equivalency diploma (GED) within two years after they would have graduated, compared to 94 percent of teen women who did not give birth. With her education cut short, a teenage mother may lack job skills, making it hard for her to find and keep a job. Therefore, she may become financially dependent on her family or on welfare. Teen mothers are more likely to live in poverty than women who delay childbearing, and nearly 75 percent of all unmarried teen mothers go on welfare within 5 years of the birth of their first child. Not only that, teens may not have good parenting skills, or have the social support systems to help them deal with the stress of raising an infant. One teen shared her account of the daily struggles she faces being a mother.

"I got pregnant a week before my 16th birthday. Now my child is one year old, and in his whole life, his father has only seen him one time. He doesn't visit. He doesn't pay child support. He doesn't do anything. I have only been out once without my child. The rest of the time he goes everywhere with me. I only get 4 hours of sleep. I wake up in the middle of the night and early in the morning to bathe him, change him, feed him and rock him to sleep. I have no money because every dollar is spent on diapers, baby food, clothes, medicine and doctor bills, leaving me with no money to spend on myself. I miss my friends. All I do is sit at home with my baby. I feel like I've missed out on the joys of simply being a teenager. Like going to the prom, parties, class trips, the skating rink, or just having fun. Don't get me wrong, I love my baby, but I wish this could have happened at 26 instead of 16."

What a hefty price to pay for a few moment of ecstasy.

ABORTION

According to a new analysis based on a survey of more than 10,000 women obtaining abortions in 2000-2001, 56% of women who obtain abortions are in their teens and twenties. Tom Coburn, a republican official, and other supporters, say that 180 schools in the U.S. are already handing out the mini-abortion pills to teens in school-based clinics. Ironically, many children can be assisted with abortions but cannot be given an aspirin unless parents are notified. What is even more troubling is that Seventy-eight percent of females who have abortions report a religious affiliation (43% Protestant, 27% Catholic and 8% other religions).

115

What a double whammy. Not only are they too young, but a significant number of them are in the church. Something is seriously wrong with this picture. What young people must realize is that the abortion procedures affect adolescents more severely than it affects adults. Adolescents are more likely to be suicidal, have poorer relationships with others and feel guilt, depression, and isolation after their abortion than their adult counterpart.

The affects of abortion among all women are just as alarming. According to the Family Planning Perspectives, abortions could increase a woman's risk of breast cancer in later years. Also, women who obtained abortions are at higher risk of being admitted to psychiatric hospitals than are women who delivered. One study revealed that women who had aborted later felt suicidal (33 percent), had flashbacks (61 percent), experienced negative reactions on the anniversary of their would-be delivery date (54 percent), and showed sexual difficulties (59 percent). In another study, 100 percent of the women reported feeling depressed, ninety-two percent felt anger, ninety-two percent felt guilt, and eighty-one percent had preoccupations with the aborted child following their abortions.

According to AGI Facts in Brief, forty-one percent of teens who become pregnant have abortions. The reasons why youth opt to have abortions vary. Three-fourths of all teens state that they cannot afford to have a baby; two-thirds say that they are not mature enough; and one-forth admit that have never used birth control.

Deuteronomy 30:19 says, "This day I call heaven and earth as witnesses against you that I have set before you life and death, blessings and curses, Now I choose life, so that you and your children may live."

Beyond sexually transmitted diseases, pregnancy and adultery, there are other negative affects of sexual intercourse among teenagers. According to the Roper/Starch Worldwide poll, fifty-four percent of teens who have had sex regretted it and wished they'd waited. Pediatrics journal has reported that sexually active girls have a six times greater risk to attempt suicide than girls who are virgins which points to the emotional stress/anxiety that many girls experience when they become sexually involved. As you can clearly see, the negative effects of premarital sex are endless.

Why Should I Wait Until Marriage?

In today's society virginity is a prehistoric concept. To be young and a virgin is shameful because it is assumed that everyone is doing it. The largest study in adult sexual behavior, conducted by the Social Organization of Sexuality-Sexual Practices in the United States, discovered that only 6.9% of men and 21% of women ages 18-59 had their first sexual intercourse experience on their wedding night. For too long sex has been seen as a casual activity that is shared between two or more willing parties. The sanctity of the act has been disregarded and ignored.

There was a time when virginity and abstinence were considered honorable and required as a standard of living. Sex was considered an extremely significant experience not to be taken lightly. The bible clearly explains the value

God places on virginity and the punishment for premarital sex. Deuteronomy 22:13-21 states:

"If a man marries a girl, then after sleeping with her accuses her of having had premarital intercourse with another man, saying, "She was not a virgin when I married her," then the girl's father and mother shall bring the proof of her virginity to the city judges. Her father shall tell them, "I gave my daughter to this man to be his wife, and now he despises her, and has accused her of shameful things, claiming that she was not a virgin when she married; yet here is the proof.' And they shall spread the garment before the judges. The judges shall sentence the man to be whipped, and fine him one hundred dollars to be given to the girl's father, for he has falsely accused a virgin of Israel. She shall remain his wife and he may never divorce her. But if the man's accusations are true, and she was not a virgin, the judges shall take the girl to the door of her father's home where the men of the city shall stone her to death. She has defiled Israel by flagrant crime, being a prostitute while living at home with her parents; and such evil must be cleansed from among you (TLB)."

During biblical days the father took great pride in the virginity of his daughter. He took on the responsibility of keeping her pure till marriage. It was honorable for a father to walk his daughter down the isle and present her to her new husband as a chaste virgin. The couple would traditionally get married in the morning and have the reception in the afternoon.

During the reception, while the family and friends were celebrating, the couple would go off to consummate their marriage (engage in sexual intercourse). The custom

118

was that the parents of the bride would provide the bed sheets or linens to the bride and groom as a gift to be used on their wedding night. During such time, the new couple would activate the covenant through sex. The husband would insert his penis into his wife's vagina, which would penetrate her hymen causing the shedding of blood. The blood would then pour onto the sheets given by the parents of the bride.

After the covenant was complete the couple would then fold the bloody sheets back up and give it to the parents of the bride. It was an important and prized possession indicating that she was a virgin. If the groom, for any reason, accused his wife of not being a virgin, the parents would then bring the sheets before the elders and plead on their daughter's behalf. If it was proven that her virginity was lost before marriage, indicated by stainless bed sheets, she would be stoned to death because she brought shame to her family by playing the whore (slut) in her father's house.

God did not play when it came to the sanctity of sexual purity. Death was the punishment for premarital sex. Though this passage of scripture dealt with the virginity of the female, God's order for sexual sanctity applies to the male as well. I Corinthians 6:18 says, *"Flee fornication..."* For God wants you to be holy and pure, and to keep clear of all sexual sin so that each of you will marry in holiness and honor – not in lustful passion as the heathen do, in their ignorance of God and his ways (1 Thessalonians 4:3-5).

God has specifically required that young people should serve as an example to all believers in word,

119

conversation, love, spirit, faith and purity. The purity that God is speaking of includes sexual purity. How can this be accomplished? Psalms 119:9 says, *"How can a young man stay pure? By reading your Word and following its rules."* We are drowning in the sea of immorality. Everywhere we look we find the temptation to lead impure lives. The psalmist asked a question that troubles us all: how do we stay pure in a filthy environment? We cannot do this on our own, but must have counsel and strength more dynamic than the tempting influences around us. Where can we find the strength and wisdom? By reading God's Word and doing what it says. It clearly says to avoid sexual temptation and remain sexually pure until marriage.

There are many benefits to living a life of abstinence, both physically and emotionally. Abstinence offers 100% protection against pregnancy and sexually transmitted diseases. Abstinence allows the appropriate time needed to get to know one another without allowing the distraction of lust to get in the way. Abstinence can also spare you heartache. Sexual intercourse is not just physical, but emotional as well. Remaining abstinent can allow the time needed to explore feelings and decide whether a person is the right choice. Sexual intercourse is only one of many ways to show your feelings and love for one another. By choosing to be abstinent, you are now free to seek other imaginative ways to express your feelings and demonstrate your love!

While choosing abstinence is the best decision, it isn't always the easiest one to make. With all of the sexual pressures that teens face to have sex, they should think about the source of that pressure and how it should be avoided and resisted. Under certain circumstances, sexual passion can override the best of intentions. Those circumstances may be as innocent and ordinary as spending time alone with the person you are in love with. The best way to avoid stumbling into sex is to make sure you are adequately prepared for any situation. Anticipate the circumstances you may find yourself in and rehearse what you will say and do.

For example, find enjoyable, sex-free activities and creative ways to express your love for a romantic partner. Acknowledge your partner's feelings by saying, "I understand you have strong sexual urges, and that's o.k., but that doesn't mean we have to have sexual intercourse." Clearly and compassionately explain your position. Tell your partner that you care for him or her but you don't want to have sex and that you'd appreciate it if he or she would respect that decision. If your partner threatens to break up with you because you won't have sex, don't try to stop him or her. Say, "I'm sorry you feel that way, but that won't make me change my mind." A partner who won't respect your wishes isn't worthy of your affection. They must understand that sexual union was not designed to initiate a relationship, but to consummate a permanently committed marriage relationship.

When young people begin to honor their bodies as temples of God and choose abstinence as a lifestyle choice, purity will prevail, diseases will perish, families will progress and sexual intercourse will be pleasing in the sight of God.

PIMPIN' From The Pulpit To The Pews

There's A Spirit In The House

The Power Of A Preying Preacher

e Secret Underworld Of Homosexuality In The Church

Teen Sexuality: Is There A Virgin In The House?

Overcoming The Lust Of The Eye

Help: My Body's Yearnin' And My Flesh Is Burnin'

Killing The Spirit In The House

CHAPTER 5

OVERCOMING THE LUST OF THE EYES

Ten o'clock was soon approaching and William was running late for his meeting. As he pulled into his complex parking lot, he jumped out of his car, slammed the door and darted up the stairs to his eighth floor duplex. Halting in front of his door long enough to catch his breath, William calmly entered his apartment. As he tenderly kissed his wife Claire on the forehead, he expressed his exhaustion from a hard day's work. "I think I'm gonna take a hot long bath to calm my nerves", William stated as he slipped into the bathroom.

As William carefully ran his bath water he noticed a flickering light coming from an apartment in the building adjacent to his own. Rather than inquiring about this unusual occurrence he quickly responded by flicking his bathroom light on and off. The peculiar episode between apartments was more than coincidental. Rather, it was a subtle sign that the coast was clear. The meeting that William was so adamant about attending did not occur in a boardroom but within the confines of his bathroom.

Stenography, legal pads, office machinery, conference calls and cubicles would not be required for this meeting. Instead, lust, lather and limbs would be the choice inventory for the evening. William and his inquisitive neighbor spent great ordeals of time admiring one another bare. Their curiosity for each other turned bathing from a customary cleansing to a spectator's sport.

Several nights a week they seductively disrobed themselves with the intent to entice one another with something they knew they could never experience. They sensually bathed themselves seeking to provide a sexual fantasy for their distant onlooker. Their water closet rendezvous would conclude with a methodic bodily stroking of a bath towel until completely dry. Then the lights would abruptly dim to adjourn the meeting.

As William lay in the bed beside his wife all he could think about was his well-known mystery woman. But how could this woman be both well known and mysterious at the same time. Well, she was mysterious because William knew not her name, occupation, family or educational background, hobbies or even the sound of her voice. However, he knew her in ways that those most familiar with her never knew her. He knew every curve, corner and crevice of her body. He knew her intimately. And what he knew severely hurt his marriage.

The more William began to dwell upon the obscurity of his naughty neighbor, the more he began to lose the desire he once had for his wife. He loved his wife but he just couldn't get this other woman out of his mind. What began as a forbidden admiration between two strangers soon became an addictive sexual affair. William was guilty of having eyes full of adultery that could not cease from sin. Infidelity had crept into his marriage even though he never laid hands upon this other woman. The only sexual organ stimulated by this woman was William's mind.

Every time William made love to his wife, he brought his neighbor into the bedroom with him. William would frequently place his neighbor's body on his wife's face. He would secretly use his wife's frame as a portal to engross himself in a sexual exchange with his bathroom buddy. William knowingly committed an adulterous act every time he made love to his wife.

William continued to massage his eyes with the beauty of another woman. From the bathroom to the bedroom, the immoral sexual ordeal resumed for several months. The more he sought after his distant lover, the more he neglected the needs and desires of his wife. Soon, their marriage began to weaken. The level of intimacy that William and Claire once shared began to diminish. Their union began to collapse right before their eyes. What was once a fulfilling marriage, quickly became an unstable bond between strangers.

But, what was the culprit that secretly entered into the confines of their sacred union? It was nothing more than a simple look. Some would argue that it was an innocent look. But was the look really innocent? Or was it a look dripping with lust? Is it possible that William forgot his Bible study lesson "thou shalt not covet thy neighbor's house" found in Exodus 20:17. Or was William's actions a deliberate act of sexual self-gratification despite all consequences? No matter how you may answer these questions, the culprit remains the same: the look of lust.

The Lust Of The Eyes

Every act of sexual sin: erotic fantasy, self and mutual masturbation, heavy petting, fornication and adultery, are conceived from a look of lust. A look that leads to lust is not one that happens by chance through a quick glance. It is premeditated and fixated. It observes, stares, and takes heed, giving in to fantasy and imagination. Simply put, the lust of the eyes is when one simply looks for too long or too often.

If we continue to allow our minds to enjoy the visions of the forbidden, we fuel the desires of temptation that gives into sin. Every time you feel compelled to take a second look at someone that you find attractive you are setting yourself up for a fall. How? It's quite simple. The more you look at someone, the easier it becomes to develop a very morbid and intense appetite for that person. A forceful craving for personal pleasure is intensified by the fixation of our eyes upon a person.

A look of lust is simply a stare of sexual starvation. I Samuel 16:7 says, "...man looks at the outward appearance, but the Lord looks at the heart (NIV)." The tendency to be overwhelmingly captivated by someone's outward appearance, without inquiring the person's real value is considered lust. Therefore, such a look is shallow, empty and superficial in nature. Unfortunately, this frivolous act demands something that is so meaningful: sexual intimacy.

Proverbs 27:20 says, "Hell and destruction are never full; so the eyes of man are never satisfied (KJV)." The scripture is clearly saying that unsatisfied eyes can lead a person and their relationship to destruction and can ultimately place someone in hell. This is a severe punishment for lustful eyes. Why? The effects of lust include slavery to sin, dissatisfaction, blocked blessings, separation from God, ruin, self-hatred and hardening of our hearts. Besides, lust is something that can never be fulfilled. It is unquenchable. It never gets enough. It is designed to strip a person of everything he has and then wipe him off the face of the earth.

Wandering Eyes Will Lead To Your Demise

"What are you looking at?", yelled Tasha, as she saw her husband gazing at a petite, young woman walking across the street. "Nothing" sighed John after hearing another accusation about the direction of his eyes. "I saw you lookin' at her! Don't stand here and lie to me. I'm sick and tired of you looking at some other woman every time I turn my head. Do you want her?"

This dialogue has become a common conversation amongst couples that suffer from a spouse's wandering eyes. Whether it be the husband or the wife, this uncontrolled behavior has negatively affected many relationships. Unfortunately, this is not a recent phenomenon. The wandering of lustful eyes goes back many centuries. It goes all the way back to the garden of Eden.

Genesis 3:1 says, "And when the woman saw that the tree was good for food, and that it was *pleasant to the eyes*, and a tree to be desired to make one wise, she took of the fruit thereof, and did eat..." Adam and Eve had rights to all that was in the garden except for the tree of good and evil. The very thing that did not belong to them became the very thing that they desired.

Unfortunately, what manifested in the garden has transcended in the daily lives of people. Rather than people desiring the fruit from of a tree, men and women have become the forbidden fruit that many now crave. Let's take a look at three biblical characters to discover how wandering eyes can lead to your demise.

Potipher's Wife

And it came to pass after these things; that his master's wife **cast her eyes upon Joseph**; and she said, Lie with me.   Genesis 39:7

Potipher's wife, by anyone's standards, would be considered well-to-do. Potipher, her husband, was a high-ranking officer to the Pharaoh of Egypt. He was a man of power, personality, and prestige. His hard work and dedication to service awarded them a spacious and luxuriously furnished home, a bountiful amount of food and clothing, as well as an abundance of wealth. Pharaoh's wife was rendered a sizable household staff that catered to her every beckon call. In essence, she wanted for nothing. She appeared to possess everything that any woman could ever hope for: a good man and a life of luxury. Externally, she was the object of every woman's envy.

However, there was a longing and craving hidden deep within the depths of her heart that led her down a very dangerous path. Potipher's wife obtained every possession but lacked her greatest obsession. Potipher. She was neglected and rejected by the one thing that once brought her joy. She was married to a man who was married to his work. As a result, he was never home, thus giving his wife very little time. So, in search for fulfillment and a sense of satisfaction, she found something to occupy her time. His name was Joseph.

Joseph was commissioned by Potipher as his top aide to care for his home. This young slave boy was entrusted with all that he had because Potipher recognized the favor of God that Joseph had upon his life. However, all that Potipher's wife chose to recognize was his incredible sex appeal. The bible says that Joseph was well built and handsome (Gen. 39:6). Daily, Joseph would innocently parade his young, attractive, well-built physique around the palace with no thought of an admirer.

Engrossed with an unfulfilled yearning for attention from an absent husband and consumed with a desire to fulfill a sexual craving, the bible says that Potipher's wife cast her eyes upon Joseph and propositioned him to indulge in a sacred ritual of oneness within the confines of her marital quarters. To cast one's eyes upon something is to select or to be assigned to that particular thing. Well, wooing Joseph into a sexual relationship became her only obsession and assignment. "Come to bed with me!" (Genesis 39:7) was the one plea that she relentlessly insisted that Joseph fulfill. She tried to get Joseph to sexually succumb to her seductive stare. " The bible says that she spoke to Joseph day after day but he refused.

Potipher's wife was a victim of wandering eye. Some scholars say that she was a sexually immoral woman with absolutely no discretion. Others categorize her as one of the many bad girls of the bible who are just scandalous in nature. However, when you study this fascinating story you will discover an absentee husband who had more concerned for the food in his belly than the wife in his own home (Genesis 39:6). Though he provided for his wife's material needs, her spiritual, emotional and possible sexual needs were neglected.

Companionship is more than a simple desire. It is an essential need. When it is missing within the confines of a relationship it can possibly lead to emptiness, and a feeling of loneliness. Unfortunately, many spouses have turned into the arms of another man or woman when felt unwanted and unappreciated within their own relationship. While the act of infidelity is totally reprehensible, it has become the common response of a neglected spouse. So it is possible that the lustful eye of Potipher's wife could have been birthed or magnified by the neglect of her spouse.

Samson

And he came up, and told his father and his mother, and said, **I have seen a woman** in Timnath of the daughters of the Philistines: now therefore get her for me to wife.

Judges 14:2

Samson was a man of enormous physical strength who was destroyed by the power of an even greater weakness. Born to deliver Israel out of the hands of the Philistines, Samson was raised as a Nazarite – a person who took a vow to be set apart for God's service. His call of God and physical strength led to many victories in battle against the Philistines.

His most applauded war stories include removing the gigantic gates of the city and carrying them away on his shoulders after ripping it off its hinges all by himself. Samson set their fields afire and ruined their crops. In one battle he slew 1,000 of the Philistines all by himself using for a weapon the jawbone of a donkey that he found on the ground nearby. Samson even strangled a lion with his bare hands.

Despite his supernatural strength and unprecedented victories, Samson will always be remembered for what he might have been. Samson was to do great things for God, but allowed his undisciplined eyes to be taken off of Him and fixated on forbidden women. Interestingly, the first recorded words of Samuel in the bible were "I saw a woman... Get her for me, for she looks good to me." Unfortunately, this infamous statement became a re-occuring act of disobedience that led to his ultimate demise.

Samson's greatest weakness was beautiful women. No matter how strong he was, he couldn't conquer the soft nature of a woman. He was attracted to the opposite sex strictly on the basis of outward appearance. He was a sucker for soft skin, a beautiful face and a feminine frame. Samson became so preoccupied with his lustful desire, he didn't know God had left him. Samson lacked spiritual discretion when it came to the women he wanted.

It was forbidden by God to marry, or even mingle, with Philistine women because of their worship of pagan gods. However, the lustful desire of Samson's eyes far surpassed his desire to please God. Despite his parent's refusal, Samson insisted on marrying a fine Philistine woman from Timnath. He later enjoyed the forbidden pleasures of Philistine prostitutes from Gaza. However, no woman could woo Samson like Delilah, a Philistine woman from the valley or Sorek.

Delilah was a beautiful woman and knew how to wear a dress to make a brother scream. Delilah proved that even strong men harbor hidden weaknesses. Night after night he spent an incalculable amount of hours with her in her home. Her charm and flawless appearance turned Samson into a hopeless romantic. Unfortunately, she was a deceitful woman with honey on her lips and poison in her heart. Pretending to love Samson, Delilah conspired with the Philistines to bring Samson to his knees in exchange for eleven hundred shekels of silver.

Delilah said to Samson, "Tell me the secret of your great strength and how you can be tied up and subdued." Now, common sense should have told Samson that Delilah was up to no good but love will make you dumb, deaf and blind and completely out of your mind. Rather than flowing in the spirit of discernment, Samson was simply stuck on stupid. Delilah made three separate attempts to discover the secret to his strength and every time, Samson misled her. However, after weeks of nagging, prodding and whining, Samson gave in. The bible states that Samson was vexed by her constant nagging. Other translations say that Samson was "annoyed to death."

Then Samson's wife threw herself on him, sobbing, "You hate me! You don't really love me..." So, with no hope for peace in his home, Judges 16:17 says that he told her everything. "No razor has ever been used on my head," he said, "because I have been a Nazarite set apart to God since birth. If my head were shaved, my strength would leave me, and I would become as weak as any other man (NIV)."

After Samson's heartfelt confession, Delilah put him to sleep on her lap. That same night, Delilah ordered the Philistine soldiers to quickly consume Samson. Shackled and shaven from a merciless legion of Philistine soldiers, Samson's strength instantly became a memory of the past. They chained him to a huge stone wheel and pulled him through the city as a conquered warrior for all the nation to see. And if that wasn't enough they blinded Samson by using a hot poker to burn his eyes out of his sockets.

Interesting, isn't it? The very thing that Samson used to get him into all this trouble was the very thing that was striped from him: his eyes. His wandering eyes led to his ultimate demise. No matter how good someone may look, never allow your eyes to cause you to disobey God.

David

And it came to pass in an eveningtide, that David arose from off his bed, and walked upon the roof of the king's house: and from the roof **he saw a woman washing herself**; and the woman was very beautiful to look upon.

2 Samuel 11:2

King David, heir to the throne of Israel, arose from his bed one evening to bathe in the glory of his kingdom. While strolling along the rooftop of his palace, he became

135

mesmerized by all that he had seen. It was not the surrounding nations that had been conquered throughout the years of David's illustrious reign. Nor was it the sacredness of the Ark of the Covenant placed within the courts of Jerusalem. What captured David's attention and had him spellbound was the beauty of a Black woman bathing. The combination of her beauty, the gentle water cascading down her curvature frame and the dancing silhouette of the evening shadows pulsating rhythmically to her every move enticed the cravings trapped within David's loins.

What began as a cursory glance soon began a lustful fixation. David's desire to have this woman would not allow him to retire to his chambers for all night prayer. Rather, he sent for her that they might indulge in a passionate exchange. Bath-sheba being the wife of Uriah, King David's most loyal soldier, meant nothing to his lustful eye. He wanted what he wanted and would stop at nothing to get it. Bath-sheba knew it was wrong to commit adultery, but to refuse a king's request could mean punishment or death.

Shortly after their one-night stand, Bath-sheba discovered that she was impregnated with a seed from a man that she barely knew. Word of the unplanned pregnancy soon got back to King David. Backed into a corner with no thought of what to do next, David chose to cover up his sin. King David ordered Uriah's death by placing him on the front line of Israel's next battle. He then married Bath-sheba so no one could discover the wickedness of his ways.

David lived a lie for an entire year before it was discerned by Nathan, a prophet and most trusted advisor to the throne. Nathan was commissioned to reveal God's judgment to David for all of his iniquities. God spoke through Nathan in 2 Samuel 12:10-12.

"Why, then, have you despised the laws of God and done this horrible deed? For you murdered Uriah and stolen his wife. Therefore murder shall be a constant threat in your family from this time on, because you have insulted me by taking Uriah's wife. I vow that because of what you have done I will cause your own household to rebel against you. I will give your wives to another man, and he will go to bed with them in public view. You did it secretly, but I will do this to you openly, in the sight of all Israel."

Although repentance followed David's behavior so did the consequences of his actions. The consequences were not just a curse upon David's life alone, but his family and the nation of Israel as well.

Mayhem spread through his family. David now faced sins in his family similar to those he had committed. The sin in his life was magnified in the lives of his children. The child that was born from David and Bath-sheba's act of infidelity surely died. Next, David's eldest son Amnon raped his half-sister Tamar and kicked her out of his home. By throwing her out, Amnon made it look as if Tamar had made a shameful proposition towards him. His crime destroyed her chances of marriage. Because she was no longer a virgin, she could not be given in marriage.

Absalom, David's third son, secretly sought vengeance against his eldest brother Amnon by the merciless shedding of his blood. Absalom fled to a distant land for three years before he returned to Jerusalem. Two years past before King David granted Absalom permission to see him. During the interim of his return and his meeting with the king, Absalom's heart turned against his father. He slowly stole the hearts of all the people of Israel and organized a rebellion against the king. David lost his kingdom and Absalom slept with many of the king's wives with the intent to publicly humiliate his father. Sleeping with any of the king's wives or concubines was a way of claiming the throne.

While David was hiding out, seeking refuge for his life, I wonder if he ever asked himself where he would be if he had never taken a look at that fine black woman bathing in the middle of the night. What about Samson? What more could he have accomplished for Israel if he never laid eyes of Delilah. How about Potipher's wife? How much better could her marriage have been if she decided never to cast her eyes upon Joseph? The possibilities are endless.

What is interesting about these three biblical characters is that they all desired someone who did not belong to them. They took their eyes off of their prize (God and/or spouse) and allowed them to wander which ultimately led to their demise.

Many allow their eyes to wander out of loneliness. Others allow their eyes to wander out of lust. The reasons are far too great to measure. However, many marriages have been ruined because of an extra-marital admiration. Countless people have gotten into fights with their spouses over a so-called innocent look. So many lives are affected when people step outside of their marital boundaries and allow others to visually entice them.

Interestingly, eye contact between people act as a form of nonverbal communication. People have the ability to transmit a multitude of thoughts and messages through their eyes. A man who looks upon a woman may say "I want you right here and right now." A woman who looks upon a man may say "I can meet your needs (sexually)." Messages can be exchanged back and forth between people without having to speak a word. Therefore, the question becomes: "What are your eyes saying?" Unfortunately, too many individuals speak sensual messages with their eyes to everyone else but their own spouse.

These disgraceful looks can cause a life of no fulfillment. When men begin to zoom in on the complexion, the hair, the face, the breasts, the thighs and the behind of another woman it creates a sexual curiosity about that woman which can never be fulfilled. When women zoom in on the complexion, the chest, the back, the behind and the groin of another man it robs her of the fulfillment that should exist within the confines of her marriage.

Not only does it leave the onlooker unsatisfied, it leaves the spouse feeling insignificant, humiliated and betrayed. A wandering eye can even create insecurities within a spouse. It can make a spouse feel as if he or she is not good enough, attractive enough or even adequate enough. If the problem is not dealt with swiftly, it can lead to a life full of strife, resentment and severe emotional detachment. So, the next time that you catch yourself gazing at someone who does not belong to you, just remember that wandering eyes will lead to your demise.

No More Window Shopping

Have you ever gone to the mall and spent hours walking in and out of department stores with absolutely no money in your pocket? Well, if you are like any of the people I grew up with, you certainly have. You didn't have a red cent or a wooden nickel to call your own, but you were lookin' at a variety of items as if you had a million dollars in your pocket. Sound familiar? Sure it does. It's called window-shopping. We've all been there. I know I have.

There I was, standing in the middle of the baddest shoe store in the Lenox Mall in Atlanta, Georgia. I was paralyzed from the lip to the hip over a pair of brown and caramel two-tone alligator shoes. When I turned the shoe over to look at the price tag it read $750. I had neither a dime in my pocket nor a dollar in the bank but I was determined to get those shoes.

Every time logic kicked in and brought me back to reality, my eyes fought their way back to those 11 ½ 's. The more I looked, the more I saw myself rockin' those gators'. My mind began to strategically place them with every matching outfit in my closet. I became to contemplate when and where I would wear them. All of these thoughts were going through my mind, with not a dollar in my pocket. My eyes began to consume something that my wallet could not handle. When the fantasy was over, I realized that the gators didn't belong to me. They belonged to someone else. So, I left the store disappointed and unsatisfied.

Window-shopping has become an American pastime. However, the showcase that many of us tamper

140

with don't display clothing, rather people. We are as intrigued by members of the opposite sex as I was with those two-tone alligator shoes. Many of us stare at people we don't belong to. And the longer we look, the greater the desire and temptation there is for us to consume what we're fixated on. Sooner or later, the fixation turns into an unfulfilled fantasy. Our eyes begin to desire something that our flesh cannot obtain.

This is why window-shopping is just no good. Many spend all day looking and admiring members of the opposite sex for the pleasure that it brings. However, it can create unwanted lust and an unmet desire. Many of us as children were taught a very valuable lesson that we failed to carry into adulthood. When we went into any store, our parents told us, "If you can't afford it, don't touch it." Well, the principle that we must live by in our adulthood is the following: "If you can't touch it, don't look at it."

Job was a man that clearly understood this principle. Job 31:1-12 clearly explains how he made the principle of 'No Window Shopping' a part of his daily activities.

"I made a covenant with my eyes not to look with lust upon a girl. I know full well that Almighty God above sends calamity on those who do. He sees everything I do, and every step I take. If I have lied and deceived – but God knows that I am innocent – or if I have stepped off God's pathway, or if my heart has lusted for what my eyes have seen, or if I am guilty of any other sin, then let someone else reap the crops I have sown and let all that I have planted be rooted out. Or if I have longed for another man's wife, then may I die, and may my wife be in another man's home, and someone else become her husband. For lust is a shameful sin, a crime that should be punished. It is a devastating fire that destroys to hell, and would root out all I have planted."

Job had not only avoided committing the great sin of adultery; he had not even taken the first step toward that sin by looking at a woman with lustful desire. What did Job understand that many of our men and women have yet to acknowledge? He understood that every form of sexual sin begins with a look. Therefore, when people respond to their sexual iniquities by saying the all too familiar cliche "It just happened", don't believe it.

Sexual sin is a three-step process. First, there is an initial look. Second comes the desire birthed from the look. Third, the illegal sexual act is derived from the inability to control the desire. So, it's a domino effect. One act affects the other until you come tumbling down. Every eye gazer should recite Job's words before they start their day. So, the next time you see that pretty, little secretary or that suave corporate executive, you will know how to handle the situation. Besides, if it's not yours, why look anyway? Make a covenant with your eyes.

You must learn how to guard your eye gate. The bible instructs us to avoid all appearances of evil. What does that mean? Well, anything that triggers our minds and bodies to desire sex should be avoided at all costs. Whether it be a person, picture or televised image, if it can cause you to sin get rid of it. Therefore, HBO and Showtime late-hour flicks, MTV and BET hip-hop and R&B porn videos, Penthouse, Hustler, Playboy and Playgirl are the worst forms of entertainment. If your visual diet is consumed with beautiful faces, large breasts, soft and wet

142

skin, protruding behinds, bulging groins, hard nipples, biceps, triceps, and rippled stomachs, it will unmistakably stimulate your mind and trigger unfulfilled bodily responses. Your eye gate should be consumed with your spouse and the word of God. Your entertainment should be tasteful and full of moral content.

The laws of Moses mentioned in Matthew 5:27-29 says:

"You shall not commit adultery,' But I say: Anyone who even looks at a woman with lust in his eye has already committed adultery with her in his heart. So if your eye – even if it is your best eye! – causes you to lust, gouge it out and throw it away. Better for part of you to be destroyed than for all of you to be cast into hell (TLB)."

Christ said that if one should be faced with losing his eye or losing his soul, it would be foolish to keep the eye. Though Christ wasn't telling us to amputate parts of our bodies, he expects us to cut off the source of our lust or to remove ourselves from the temptation. One major way to accomplish this task is to agree to 'No More Window Shopping'.

Seek Ye My Face

Every husband or wife who has secretly suffered from a spouse with wandering eyes, has cried a simple prayer reverberated over and over again: 'Seek Ye My Face'. Though it sounds like a simple request, it has proven to be a major challenge for many. However, no spouse should knowingly seek to find pleasure in the beauty of another person.

If one is careful not to look at members of the opposite sex while in the presence of their spouse, the same courtesy should be extended in their absence. Besides, would you want your spouse all up in somebody else's face every time you turn a corner? Of course not. Proverbs 6:25 says, "Lust not after her beauty in thine heart; neither let her take thee with her eyelids." This scripture is written for women alike.

Anyone who has trouble with wandering eyes should study the sport of horse racing. Every horse is given blinders before the start of any derby. The blinders keep the horse from looking in any direction other than the finish line. Blinders leave room for no distraction. Similarly, God requires the same of us. Proverbs 4:25 says, "Let thine eyes look right on, and let thine eyelids look straight before thee." Looking straight ahead with your eyes fixated on your prize, keeps you from getting sidetracked on detours that lead to temptation.

The bible offers a blueprint for all men and women who desire to keep their eyes on their prize. First, let's take a look at the book of Psalms. In the 27th division of Psalms, David expresses his earnest desire to seek God's face. Verse 4 says, "One thing have I desired of the Lord, that will I seek after, that I may dwell in the house of the Lord all the days of my life, to behold the beauty of the Lord, and to inquire in his temple." When you skip down to verse 8 it reads, "When thou said, Seek ye my face, my heart said unto thee, Thy face, Lord will I seek."

David sought to develop a more intimate relationship with God by seeking His face. Man's relationship with God is simply a foreshadowing of what our relationship with one another should be. The same love and behavior that we exhibit before God should be extended to our mates as well. Therefore, let us now take the same scriptures found in the book of Psalms and replace the word 'Lord' with the word 'spouse'.

Verse 4 would read "One thing have I desired of my spouse, that will I seek after, that I may dwell in the house of my spouse all the days of my life, to behold the beauty of my spouse, and to inquire in his (her) temple (home)." Verse 8 would read, "When thou said, Seek ye my face, my heart said unto thee, Thy face, spouse will I seek." What a powerful mirror image of our love toward God extended toward our mates. Therefore, we can learn how to seek the face of our spouse, as well as continue to seek the face of our Lord.

In order for this principle to work, both the onlooker and the one being sought have a specific role to play. The onlooker must agree to make a covenant with his eyes and to behold the beauty of his spouse. However, the one being sought must step up to the plate as well. The bible depicts God as 'the beauty of the Lord'. That means that God is beautiful. Therefore, spouses should do their best to maintain their beauty as well.

Williard Harley Jr., author of *His Needs Her Needs: Building An Affair Proof Marriage,* lists an attractive spouse as one of the five most important emotional needs within a marriage. Attractiveness is one of the most important contributions that one can make to guarantee a spouse's happiness. A person with a need for an attractive spouse feels good whenever they look at their attractive spouse.

A common trait amongst many wives in the bible was their stunning beauty. Sarai, Abraham's wife, was so beautiful that Abraham asked her to tell the Egyptians that they were siblings. He feared that if the Egyptians knew of their marital status they would kill him in order to obtain Sarai for themselves. Esther, The wife of King Ahasuerus, was chosen from among 1,000 women as the most beautiful woman in the kingdom. The bible says that the king was so pleased with her that he crowned her as queen and offered to give her half the kingdom upon her request. Rachel, the wife of Jacob, was also known for her beauty. Jacob was so in love and captivated by her beauty that he worked a sum total of 14 years in order to wed Rachel. Now that's beautiful.

Men have gone to great lengths to obtain beautiful women as their wives. Unfortunately, many wives start to put on weight, dress less becoming or fail to maintain their overall attractiveness after marriage. Most men have a significant need for an attractive spouse. By taking care of your physical appearance, you are taking care of your husband.

Unfortunately, too many men have been known to stray once their wives no longer met their need for physical attraction. Therefore, it is your job to help keep your husband's eyes from wandering. Whatever you did to initially win him over, is what you must continue to do to keep him. So, take that house-on-the-prairie burlap dress off and throw those big mama night gowns away.

Wives, you must become your husband's super model and cover girl. Victoria's Secret and Frederick's of Hollywood should be your home away from home. Break out the Revlon'. Tantalize his eyes. Seduce him. Mesmerize him. You have been given a special power by God to knock him to his knees. Don't keep your power locked up in a closet for a rainy day. Use it and make it last forever. Give him no excuse to ever desire any other woman.

Make that man want to come home. Become his fantasy. Be creative. Put pin-ups of you all around the house. Put on sexy lingerie and dance for him. Maintain that nice shape that you have as best as you can. Keep your hair done. Wear clothes that compliment your physique. Allow your husband to stare at your body. You must always remember that men are sight stimulated, so you must remain the center of his attraction.

Husbands have a responsibility as well. In order for every wife to truly desire her husband, he must make himself desirable in her sight. Discover what it is that turns your woman on, and try your best to line up with that expectation. Always try to dress for her. A t-shirt and shorts are good for around the house but try to be presentable in public.

Generally, women are sticklers for personal hygiene. Make it your business to always maintain a bodily odor that is pleasurable to the nose. Soap, deodorant and cologne are an absolute must. Remember, funky feet and tart breath are a major turn off. Crest, a mouthful of scope and a tic-tac can work wonders.

Maintain a well-groomed appearance as well. Ashy is not classy. Always keep your hands and knees soft and lubricated with lotion. Frequently, clip your toenails. There's nothing worse than turning a playful act of footsy into a full combat sport. Go to the salon and get a manicure and pedicure every once in while. The key is maintenance. If you can keep up with your appearance, you can win her heart and eyes every time.

Many spouses believe that the need for attractiveness is based upon immaturity and a shallow sense of values. They also believe that one should look beyond a spouse's appearance. Well, that's exactly what will happen. Your spouse may possibly look right beyond your appearance to admire the appearance of another. Beauty is in the eye of the beholder. Therefore, it is important to try your best to look the way your spouse likes you to look so he or she doesn't feel tempted to behold the beauty of another. Ask your spouse for an honest appraisal of your overall physical appearance and do your best to accommodate your spouse's wishes. Remember, the goal is to keep your spouse's eyes on you because wandering eyes will lead to the relationship's demise.

PIMPIN' From The Pulpit To The Pews

There's A Spirit In The House

The Power Of A Preying Preacher

The Secret Underworld Of Homosexuality In The Church

Teen Sexuality: Is There A Virgin In The House?

Overcoming The Lust Of The Eye

Help: My Body's Yearnin' And My Flesh Is Burnin'

Killing The Spirit In The House

CHAPTER 6

HELP: MY BODY'S YEARNIN' & MY FLESH IS BURNIN'

Malik was a very successful thirty-three year-old massage therapist with seven years of experience under his belt. He specialized in releasing stress and tension from the female body in order to build up muscle for maximum performance. Starting as a small independent masseur, Malik hustled his way into contract work with chiropractor offices and spa resorts. After gaining a personal clientele, he decided to venture off and form his own company.

New to the city of Atlanta, he soon discovered that strip clubs were prominent within its city limits. No stranger to the club scene himself, he knew that many women both worked or visited such establishments. Determined to make his mark, Malik convinced club owners to allow him to set-up a chair in the clubs for female dancers.

It turned out to be an instant success. Not only did he solicit work from dancers but customers as well. Soon, personal rubdowns turned from weekly club appearances to personal house calls.

Malik exercised more liberty within the homes of his clients than he could within a public facilities. Massage tables, linens, incense, oils and sultry music completed his repertoire. Strictly professional with each of his clients, he determined within himself not to be swayed by the beauty of his clientele. However, each woman had a different motive in mind. They knowingly made each movement of his hands sensual rather than therapeutic. With women teasingly but forcefully moving his hands in forbidden territories, this made his job all the more challenging. Once the service was provided, Malik firmly resolved he would never return. But with a handsome earning potential and a deep-rooted attraction for several of his clients, he decided to return.

Unknown to him, these same women chose to raise the stakes during their private session. Once the massage was completed and paid for, quite a few dropped an extra $100 bill on the table for an erotic massage that would culminate into sexual intercourse. The same 'strictly professional' Malik who started with the best of intentions soon became a weak-willed sole proprietor with nothing to lose. By the end of his third month in the business he slept with ten 'professional' clients.

Full of a confidence that was equally parallel to his talent, Malik skillfully used his profession as a masseur to solicit sex with 40 other women through the practice of sensual massage. Eighty percent of these 40 women were reoccurring partners. Most of his relationships started off on a table and ended in between the sheets of a bed. Group sex, ménage a trios and sex with animals (snakes) also made his list of sexual accomplishments.

After time, what was once completely fulfilling to him soon became unrewarding. He slept with so many women that he lost all passion for it. Each sexual experience made him more empty and shallow. It no longer fulfilled him. He began to long for something that no woman could satisfy. He wanted to feel something that no woman could physically touch. In the depths of his internal despair, he sought after God.

Malik, in an attempt to turn his life around, chose to declare a life of celibacy. His heartfelt declaration lasted a mere month. He wanted a change but wasn't willing to give up the very thing that led to his downfall: massage therapy. Five women later, he once again yearned for a change to occur. He began to go to church regularly and eventually got saved. He thought life would be different but, to his surprise, it wasn't. His heart changed but his choice of profession and clientele remained the same. Malik had spurts of celibacy, one month here, two months there. But his job considerably compromised his relationship with God. Women remained his weakness.

During brief periods of celibacy, sexual cravings would kick in like an addiction. He suffered many restless nights. Tossing and turning with thoughts of Karen, Shalonda, Denise, Sinclair, Michele and Melanie, running through his mind, were too much for him to handle. Flashbacks of personal encounters and fantasies of unconquered territory led to a secret life of compulsive masturbation. Midnight calls were often made to women who were available at a moment's notice. And once again he found himself right back into what he desperately tried so hard to get out of. He trained his body for sex and knew not how to break the vicious cycle of lust.

It was no longer him acting out of order. Rather, there was something controlling him; a power; a spirit; an unshakable force he had no control of. Today, that same sexual stronhold continues to dwell within the depths of his loins. Sadly, having developed no control over his flesh, the saga continues...

Hijacked by A Sexual Compulsion

The church is overwhelmed with people from various social, economic, educational and spiritual backgrounds who struggle with the plague of sexual sin. Ironically, church positions have nothing to do with one's level of spiritual maturity. There are many ushers, choir members, pastor assistants, musicians, deacons, elders and even preachers who are hijacked by a sexual compulsion. These are individuals who struggle with an irresistible impulse to act upon their sexual desires, regardless of how irrational the motivation. These are churchgoers who are not easily identifiable. They are devout tithe payers. They are gifted in words of wisdom, healing and the interpretation of tongues. They serve on several ministries. They are excited about Christ. They are single. They are married. They are young. They are old. They represent every spectrum of the church. However, they are forcibly manipulated by an internal struggle that continually pulls them down into the depths of sexual despair.

While in church, the pre-occupation to serve the Lord is evident. Declarations to be sold out for Christ are often made. The power to tread on serpents is often felt. But once the benediction is given, temptation, erotic thoughts and a burning sexual desire is waiting right outside the church doors. It's a completely different reality. The desire to please the lord and our flesh is ever present. What a paradox.

Both the flesh and the spirit want to be gratified. However, they are in complete opposition to one another. The spirit's sole purpose is to obey God. That's it. That's all. There's no other function for the spirit. The flesh, on the other hand, serves the law of sin. It is corrupt and unchanging. It cannot be improved or bettered in any way. The flesh is hostile to God. It does not and cannot submit to God's law.

Many Christians have allowed their flesh to control them, thus making the spirit subject to its power. Many engage in persistent and escalating patterns of sexual behavior acted out despite increasing consequences to themselves and others. They have allowed their flesh to steer them into a life of: compulsive masturbation, multiple affairs, constant use of pornography, unsafe sex, multiple or anonymous sex partners, phone sex, cyber sex, sexual massage and prostitution. Yes, I'm referring to people in the church. Unfortunately, these sexual activities have sabotaged relationships, careers, self-esteem and life itself.

Many Christians have used sex as a means to cope with problems, handle boredom, anxiety and other powerful feelings. Others have used it as a way to feel important, wanted or powerful. These aforementioned sexual activities

155

keep people in bondage. Most find themselves wrapped in a web of lies and manipulation, consistently hiding from those close to them, while using justification, rationalization and outright denial to lie to themselves. The sexual compulsion causes them to act in ways that go against their values and beliefs. Even worse, many Christians with a flesh problem frequently say to themselves, "This is the last time that I am going to ..." yet they often find themselves feeling driven to return to the same sexual situations despite previous commitments to change. Most carnal led Christians are often unable to make and keep commitments to themselves and others about stopping or changing particular sexual behaviors over the long-term. They just continue to ride down the fast lane of sexual sin in the passenger's seat while lust recklessly drives at full force.

Enslaved By Masturbation

Masturbation remains a sore spot that causes an enormous amount of ambiguity within the body of Christ. There are two schools of thought concerning this self-stimulating activity. Many have made the argument that the bible never speaks about masturbation. Therefore, if it is not mentioned it certainly cannot be wrong. Others have manipulated scripture in order to plead their case, whether pro or con. In order for us to determine the spiritual legality of such an act we must truly understand what the act is and search the scriptures for an answer.

Webster's Dictionary defines masturbation as erotic stimulation especially of one's own genital organs commonly resulting in orgasm and achieved by manual or other bodily contact exclusive of sexual intercourse, by instrumental manipulation, occasionally by sexual fantasies, or by various combinations of these agencies. Well, it is obvious that masturbation is a very sexual act. Now the question remains, "What does the bible have to say about masturbation?"

It is the word of God that instructs us on how to conduct our body. 1 Thessalonians 4:3-5 says: *"For this is the will of God, that you should be consecrated (separated and set apart for pure and holy living): that you should abstain and shrink from all sexual vices (sin), That each one of you should know how to possess (control, manage) his own body in consecration (purity, separated from things profane) and honor, Not [to be used] in the passion of lust like the heathen, who are ignorant of the true God and have no knowledge of His will (TLB)."*

According to this scripture, the bible is clear on how we are to view masturbation. The scripture said abstain from all sexual vices (habits). Fornication, adultery, homosexuality, loose and unclean conduct and masturbation are all examples of sexual vices. While some Christians abide by the scripture concerning fornication and adultery, many struggle with masturbation. Masturbation has always been a dirty little secret hidden behind the veils of individuals' private lives. Ironically, people would rather confess a promiscuous lifestyle than a habitual act of self-indulgence. For years, masturbation has been noted solely as a male activity. However, with a shift in societal norms, more and more women are admitting to the once detestable act of masturbation. National polls, surveys and statistics report that men and women are neck in neck with their acceptance and practice of the activity.

Masturbation has become the new form of sex for the individual practicing abstinence. In short, it is solo sex. Christians who fornicate often feel the emotions of shame and guilt during and after indulging in a sex act. Similarly, shame and guilt are attached to masturbation. Therefore, whether single or married, the act can never be God's plan for his people. Whether you casually masturbate or suffer from an addiction, the results can be potentially devastating.

Compulsive masturbation with or without the use of pornography presents longstanding problems. Whether it is through cyber-sex, phone sex, videos, porn-magazines or simply through fantasy, people can often lose hours daily to the isolating activity of masturbation. Those involved in compulsive masturbation may lead lonely disconnected lives, never really understanding what it is that keeps them from real intimacy and connection with those around them. Caught in compulsive patterns, often begun in childhood or adolescence, the individual who masturbates compulsively may masturbate every night before bedtime or every morning in the shower. Thus, this behavior becomes as much a part of their daily routine as eating or sleeping.

No matter how creatively one masturbates, masturbation remains a temporary fix that cannot satisfy. It's a short-lived experience that keeps one coming back for more. It's a thirst that can never be quenched. However, it is more than just a physical longing. It is more of an appetite of the mind. The mind is the place where the imagination resides. It is also the largest sexual organ in the body. The act of masturbation forces the mind to relive past sexual experiences or envision future fantasies. It is the mental stimulation that brings an individual to climax. Therefore, when you masturbate you become a slave to your carnal (sensual) mind. The Bible declares that carnality leads to spiritual death because a lustful mind is complete hatred towards God.

The biblical solution to controlling the mind is found in 2 Corinthians 10:5. *"Casting down imaginations, and every high thing that exalteth (elevates) itself against the knowledge of God, and bringing into capacity every thought to the obedience of Christ (KJV)."* If the Bible says to think on pure things and you're imagining what sex would be like with someone, that thought has to be brought into captivity. All lustful thoughts that are contrary to the word of God must be quickly destroyed. So, in order to truly conquer and destroy the spirit of masturbation, you must simply starve your flesh and feed your spirit.

The following is an account of a young man's struggle with masturbation and his ultimate triumph.

"For six years I have struggled with the spirit of lust. I was never a really promiscuous man, but the desire for sex kept me trapped in a self-destructive behavior. Understanding that sex was off limits until marriage, I often settled for the next best thing, masturbation. It was an excessive, compulsive habit that often drove me to the point of no possible return. Masturbation was a drug my body craved for. I often compared myself to Pookie, in

New Jack City, simply because the drug that I had eternally been addicted to kept calling me. Anything that remotely reminded me of the pleasures of sex, resulted in a self-stimulating one-man-show. Late-night movies, girly magazines, sexually explicit music, music videos and large breasts drove me into the wiles of physical pleasure. Vaseline, lotion, naked pin-ups, porn tapes and a vast imagination were the tools I used to meet my sexual high.

My dirty deed was not limited to a late-night visitation within the solitude of my own home. On the contrary, it accompanied me at all times, spaces and places. It followed me into public bathroom stalls, street alleyways, behind parked cars, woodsy areas and even in gridlock traffic. While people often left non-smoking public areas to inhale a soothing but fatal nicotine stick, I often left public premises to relieve a burning fire sparked from within. Though the pleasurable indulgence soothed the savage beast that lay within, it often caused me to drop to my knees in guilt, pity and shame. That's not all. My eyes, knees, and spine weakened which caused me tremendous physical harm. I cried out for help, but no force was strong enough to rescue me from my own deplorable pit of destruction. I tried almost everything but nothing seemed to work. But it wasn't until I emersed myself in the Word of God that changes began to take place. The scripture convicted me and gave me a step-by-step solution for finally overcoming a habit that could have ultimately destroyed my life. The scripture will never be able to kill the urge and craving that periodically seeks to consume my body, but it can stop the lascivious spirit in its path and declare it defeated in the name of Jesus."

Haunted By A Secret Thought Life

Are you leading a secret thought life significantly different from the one that is known by others? If your thoughts were audible, would you be embarrassed if others knew what was going on in your mind? Countless single Christians are mentally preoccupied with sex. When a child is told not to touch something, the first thing he does when the parent is not around is touch it. Why? The curiosity of why he can't touch it motivates him. Likewise, many singles are either curious about the forbidden act of pre-marital sex or reminiscent of their sexual past. Which ever may apply, the mind is the tool that is used to trigger the sexual response.

The mind initiates the act of masturbation. The mind triggers the act of fornication. The mind convinces one to indulge in an extra-marital affair. The mind leads some down the wayward path of homosexuality. Every sexual act, whether bad or good, is significantly influenced by the mind.

Sadly, many are enslaved by the power of their mind. They are haunted by a secret thought life that sexually manipulates their behavior. There's an old adage that says, "An idle mind is the devil's workshop." A workshop is a small room where work is done. Well, you can employ the devil through your thoughts and allow him to set up shop in your mind. Interestingly, the devil's greatest weapon is in the power of suggestion, the process by which one thought or mental image leads to another.

Satan resides in your mind with three buttons to push to keep you perpetually bound in guilt, shame and sexual

161

immorality. He has a memory playback, rewind and fantasy button. Every act that you've engaged in, pornographic image that you've seen, and unmet sexual desire that you've had can be manipulated by Satan in the form of an erotic memory or sexual fantasy. However, we are at fault when we entertain the thoughts that Satan injects in our minds.

The devil is slick at what he does. Out of nowhere a thought can be put into your mind. You can be in Sunday morning service in the middle of worship, and Satan can flash an image of a half-naked video hottie from a P. Diddy video on BET. Unfortunately, you entertain the thought and it knocks you right out of worship. You may be sitting next to your husband in service, but your mind is fixated on the fine gentlemen a pew in front of you that you met in the parking lot last Sunday.

Many may think that a secret thought life isn't a sin. Besides, it's not hurting anyone. It's just a thought. That thinking is far from the truth. A simple thought triggered by glimpsing at a sexy person, seeing an erotic movie or reading an erotic story can lead you down the path of the forbidden. Giving attention as well as entertaining a simple thought can grow into a more elaborate fantasy. Fantasy can trigger sexual arousal. Once sexually aroused, the desire to feed that arousal may aggressively be pursued and fulfilled.

Each of us leads a secret thought life, an invisible life known only to us. The question is, "what are you thinking?" Genesis 11:6 says, *"...and now nothing will be restrained from them, which they have imagined to do."* This scripture speaks to how powerful your mind really is. Bruce

Wilkinson, author of *Victory Over Temptation*, shares a story of a pastor's struggle with lustful thoughts.

"Another pastor had been struggling with lustful thoughts toward a college girll in his church. Rather than dealing with his struggles alone with the Lord, with a mature brother, or with his wife, he took the girl out to lunch to talk with her. Citing the biblical mandate to confess our sins and make things right with the person we've wronged, he told her, "I've been having lustful thoughts about you, and I felt I needed to confess them to you." Embarrassed but flattered, the girl began to entertain her own thoughts toward him, and finally they became sexually involved."

If a pastor can fall as a result of a secret thought life, what makes you think that you can not. The bible clearly states that God will judge us for everything we do, including every hidden thing, good or bad. Therefore, learn to set your mind on good and spiritual things. When Satan tries to insert illegal erotic thoughts in your mind, cancel it out by thinking about things from above.

True Deliverance

Unfortunately, for many, deliverance within the body of Christ has been nothing more than a complete fiasco. The altar experience has consisted of a whole lot of shakin' and quakin', rollin', shoutin', tears droppin', and snot poppin' theatrics. Interestingly, when all of the jerkin' comes to an end, many return to their seats feeling totally delivered. However, once the benediction is given, many run right out of the church back into what they've just gotten out of. And the following Sunday they wind up in the same prayer line seeking deliverance for the same thing.

This vicious cycle continues for years because many have not come to understand the meaning of true deliverance. Deliverance is not a unilateral but a binary contract between you and God. Put simply, God has a responsibility in your deliverance. And you have a responsibility in your deliverance. Neither is your desire or God's might alone, enough to receive deliverance. It truly takes the both of you working together to bring forth complete deliverance.

Churches are full of people in desperate situations running to the altar in order to receive a touch from the pastor. Eagerly anticipating a touch of healing, deliverance and restoration, many spiritually hungry souls cry out asking God to fix them. "Change me Lord!" "Fix my problem and make it go away!" They believe and stand on the Word, but don't live the Word concerning deliverance. Unfortunately, many saints are guilty of waiting for God to do something for us instead of along with us.

The scriptures are clear about the role that the Lord plays in our deliverance. John 8:36 says, *"If the Son therefore shall make you free, ye shall be free indeed."* 2 Corinthians 3:17 says, *"...And where the Spirit of the Lord is, there is liberty."* It is quite clear that we are set free through the awesome power of God's spirit. However, once we are free, it becomes our responsibility to remain free. But how can we remain totally free and delivered from Satan's sexual snare.

The only way to overcome lust and live a sexually pure life is to walk in the spirit. Galatians 5:16 says, "*Walk in the Spirit, and ye shall not fulfill the lust of the flesh.*" To walk in the spirit means to walk in the word of God. Psalms 119:9 asks, "*How can a young man cleanse his way? By taking heed according to Your word.*" It goes on to say in the eleventh verse, "*Your word I have hidden in my heart, that I might not sin against you.*" God's word not only purifies us from sin, it also prevents sinful behavior.

Romans 6:12,13 instructs us on how to relate to sin: "*Therefore, do not let sin reign in your mortal body that you should obey its lust, and do not go on presenting the members of your body to sin as instruments of unrighteousness; but present yourselves to God as those alive from the dead, and your members as instruments of righteousness to God.*" Your old evil desires were nailed to the cross with him; that part of you that loves to sin was crushed and fatally wounded, so that your sin-loving body is no longer under sin's control, no longer needs to be a slave to sin; for when you are deadened to sin you are freed from all its allure and its power over you. (Romans 6:6-7 TLB).

Reading and meditating on the word of God day and night will cause your mind to be renewed. No longer will it be carnal in nature, but spiritual. Your mind will line up and agree with the laws of the book and obedience will ultimately follow. Make a habit of reading the word continuously so that you will be able to successfully walk in the spirit. As you read the Word of God, it will map out a step-by-step plan to walk in sexual purity.

165

Sexual Purity: The Road Less Traveled

Ironically, the church has done an appalling job teaching people how to break free from the chains of sexual bondage. Many have preached an ineffective doctrine of do and don'ts. 'Don't do this and don't do that because the bible says so' is the warning that members often receive. Then we wonder why the church is not delivered. We wonder why fornication, incest, rape, sodomy, adultery, teenage pregnancy and broken families have entered into the church. It's simple. There are very few churches that effectively teach on the subject of sex.

Meanwhile, many saints suffer from the 'my spirit is willing but my flesh is weak' syndrome. Romans 7:18 says, *"For I know that in me (that is in my flesh), dwelleth no good thing: for to will is present with me; but how to perform that which is good I find not."* Simply put, the Apostle Paul is saying 'I know the right thing to do but I don't know how to do it.' Truthfully, many in the body of Christ want to do the right thing. However, their struggle is not knowing what to do or how to do it.

Sex is not dealt with in the church. It's been considered inappropriate. There has been no sex education in the church. Interestingly 57% of kids say they learn about sex from the movies. Seventy-three percent said they learned next to nothing from the church. The church has swept it under the carpet with attempts to hide it, hoping that it would just go away. However, sex has rushed in the church like a flood because we have not lifted up a standard against it.

Church mothers and fathers talk about the sin of fornication, but they don't teach their single members how to enter into a lifestyle of celibacy. The reality of a celibates' life is that the feelings of horniness and loneliness don't go away. How do you effectively cope with those feeling without succumbing to them. Keeping your nose stuck in your bible and just saying no to sex is simply not enough. In order to have victory over the flesh you must deny yourself and take up your cross daily. The following are the biblical steps that you must take in order to overcome the vicious cycle of sexual compulsion.

Step #1) Make A Quality Decision

In order to truly conquer the sexual struggle to stay pure, the first step that must be made is a quality decision to end all sexual behavior. However, first you must acknowledge your behavior as sin. Unfortunately, many people don't talk about sins today; they talk about problems. The reason that problems are more convenient than sins is simply because people don't have to do anything about them. If you have a problem, you can get sympathy for it, understanding for it, and even professional help for it, to name a few. Sins, on the other hand, have to be repented of, confessed and forsaken. You can put away the sinful habits that have mastered you if you truly desire to do so. You must accept your personal responsibility for them. It is ultimately up to you to determine whether you're going to let your body be used for sin or for righteousness.

In the world of boxing, when a decision is determined, one athlete is made victor over his or her opponent. Thus, the opponent becomes a victim.

Therefore, when you make a decision, you are making something victor at the expense of something else. Deuteronomy 30:19 says, "I call heaven and earth to record this day against you, that I have set before you life and death, blessing and cursing: therefore choose life, that both thou and thy seed may live:" In this scripture, life and blessings are being made the victor over death and curses. In your life you will have to make a daily quality decision regarding the flesh. Will you allow the your flesh to become the victor and your spirit the victim. Or will you allow the spirit to be the victor and the flesh the victim. The choice is yours. However, a choice must be made.

Without a quality decision being made, it's easy to be delivered from sexual sin just to find yourself right back into what you've just got out of. It's important to understand that your death to sin has finally ended your relationship with sin as master, but it hasn't terminated its existence. Sin is still alive, strong and appealing, but its power and authority have been broken (Romans 8:2). Furthermore, your flesh did not die either. You will still have memories, habits, conditioned responses, and thought patterns ingrained in your mind that will prompt you to focus on your own sexual interests and desires. Though you are no longer in the flesh, you can choose at any moment to walk according to your flesh, complying with those old urges to satisfy yourself instead of God.

The thrill of sexual calisthenics may never go away. The desire to be loved and feel romantic may always exist. No one promised that the feelings would go away. But, regardless of what your body may cry for, the quality decision of abstinence must still be made. Simply put, promiscuity is never beneficial. It is not beneficial to have sex with someone, hoping that a commitment will follow. It is not beneficial to have sex with someone you barely know. It is not beneficial to use sex as a way to get to know someone. It is not beneficial to use sex to experience instant intimacy. It is not beneficial to use sex in an attempt to hold on to someone. It is not beneficial to engage in sexual relations with a person just because it feels good.

Promiscuity is a behavior that will often leave you torn, broken, emotionally drained, resentful, cynical, untrusting and spiritually depleted. Though, the physical act may possibly give a pleasurable experience, the ramifications of such activity makes the act not worth it. So, make a quality decision today to avoid the lust of your flesh and choose celibacy.

Step #2) Guard Your Gates

Are you guilty of living a secret thought life? Would you be embarrassed if others knew what went on inside your mind? Each of us leads a secret thought life, an invisible life known only to God and ourselves. For some of us, our secret thought life consists of a dream world of fantasies that concoct intricate plans that fulfill lustful desires. Others of us fabricate chance meetings with beautiful women or handsome men who seduce us. We each invent secret images of what we want, which we would be embarrassed for others to know. Unless we develop a solid understanding of how our thoughts, motives, and ambitions are shaped, we will have impure secret thoughts, wrong motives, and selfish ambitions. If we don't leave a gatekeeper posted at the gates that lead to our inner being, then the enemy can slip into our thoughts under the cover of low awareness.

Second Corinthians says, "*We must take captive every thought to make it obedient to Christ* (NIV)." Why, you may ask? Ecclesiastes 12:14 says, "*For God will bring every deed into judgment, including every hidden thing (our secret thought life), whether it is good or evil* (NIV)." Our prayer should be the prayer of King David "*Search me, O God, and know my heart; test me and know my anxious thoughts. See if there is any offensive way in me, and lead me in the way everlasting* (Psalms 139:23,24)."

There is a very strategic way of controlling our thought life and purifying our minds. We must become gatekeepers. Each of us possess gates that allow information to enter into our minds, whether positive or negative. These gates are the eye gate, ear gate and mouth gate. Once these gates are properly guarded, the struggle for sexual purity weakens significantly.

First, you must guard your eye gate. The Bible instructs us to avoid all appearances of evil. What does this mean? Well, anything that triggers our minds and bodies to desire sex should be avoided at all costs. Therefore, HBO and Showtime late-hour flicks, graphic music videos, and porn magazines may not be the best way to entertain you. If your visual diet is consumed with beautiful faces, large breasts, soft and wet skin, protruding behinds, bulging groins, hard nipples, biceps, triceps, and rippled stomachs, it will unmistakably stimulate your mind and trigger bodily responses causing hard erections and moist appetites. Your eye gate should be consumed with the word of God.

Your entertainment should be tasteful and full of moral content.

Second, you must guard your ear gate. The bible says that evil communication corrupts good manners. Therefore, you must be careful what is being communicated to you on a regular basis. Sexually explicit lyrics should be avoided. Music has the potential of creating an atmosphere and mood that is conducive for sexual intimacy. Furthermore, you should guard your ears from stand-up comedy that is very sexual in nature. Conversing with others about their sexual experiences is also a very dangerous activity to engage in. Your ears should be consumed with the word of God, in the form of preaching, teaching and spiritual music that seeks to edify your spirit rather than provoke your flesh.

Thirdly, you must guard your mouth gate. The Bible says from the issues of the heart, the mouth speaks. What this means is that whatever you feed the heart and mind of a man, will eventually come out of his mouth. Your conversation should be pure in nature. The Bible instructs that the word of God and godly things should constantly be spoken from your mouth. Only that which is edifying should be spoken to yourself and others. By controlling all of these gates, your mind should be clear from sexual perversion, fantasy and memory.

Step #3) Rehearse the Consequences of Sexual Sin

Few people ever focus on the possible consequences of their actions. They carelessly indulge in sexual activity and deal with consequences as they arise. Unfortunately, such irresponsible behavior can be both spiritually and physically devastating. Spiritually speaking, the Bible is clear in its punishment for sexual immorality. James 1:15 says, *"Then after desire (lust) has conceived, it gives birth to sin; and sin, when it is full-grown, gives birth to death (NIV)."* The death that the scripture is referring to is first and foremost a spiritual death, which can also result in a physical death.

All sin is equal, however, they all have different consequences. I Corinthians 6:18 says, *"Every sin that a man doeth is without the body; but he that committeth fornication sinneth against his own body (KJV)."* Therefore, there is a major distinction between sin and the sin of the body. It bears much different consequences.

The best examples of consequences of sexual sin are found in the life story of King David. David gazed from his palace roof and saw a beautiful married woman bathing and lust filled his heart. He should have left the roof and fled the temptation. Instead, he entertained the temptation by indulging in a sexual affair with Bath-sheba. Though David sought God's forgiveness a year later and repented for his act of adultery, ramifications still occurred. The following are a list of the consequences that followed David's act of indiscretion.

- Consequence #1: Bath-sheba became pregnant.
- Consequence #2: David killed Uriah, Bath-sheba's husband, in order to hide his sin.
- Consequence #3: David and Bath-sheba's baby dies shortly after its birth.
- Consequence #4: David's daughter Tamar is raped by her half-brother Amnon.

- Consequence #5: David's third son Absalom avenges his sister's abuse by killing Amnon.
- Consequence #6: Absalom overthrows David's rule and takes the throne as king.
- Consequence #7: Absalom humiliates David by sleeping with his wives and concubines.
- Consequence #8: Absalom is killed in battle.

Look at this. David's one act resulted in four people being killed, one raped, a number of wives forced into the act of adultery, and an entire nation overthrown. Those are some serious consequences. The sexual sin of David did not only affect him but it affected an entire generation of people. So, if you think what you do behind closed doors is no one else's business but your own, you are wrong. The act can be devastating and the consequences are endless. The following is a partial list of possible consequences for sexual sin:

Unplanned pregnancy	Incest
Single mothers	Molestation
Juvenile delinquents	Sodomy
Families on welfare	STD's
Abortion	Guilt
Broken families	Shame
Broken hearts	Sexual baggage
Divorce	Insecurities
Emotional trauma	Fear
Broken families	Death
Rape	Hell

Imagine how different the world would be without all of these traumatic consequences. By regularly rehearsing the possible consequences of sexual sin, it will help stifle physical behavior.

Step #4) Establish Proper Boundaries

If you understand what boundaries are and do, they can be one of the most helpful tools in your life. We've learned from Dr. Henry Cloud and Dr. John Townsend's book, Boundaries in Dating, that a boundary is a property line. It distinguishes the difference between your personal property and the property of others. Though we cannot see our boundaries, we can certainly tell when someone has crossed them. When someone gets too close or persuades us to do something we don't think is right, our boundaries have been crossed. When we don't have clear limits, we expose ourselves to unhealthy and destructive influences and people. Boundaries protect us by letting others know what we will and will not tolerate.

One of the major things boundaries do is help us control how we conduct ourselves in relationship. The following are a number of boundaries that must exist in relationships in order to pursue sexual purity.

A) Avoid Being Alone

Exclusivity has got to be the number one reason for physical intimacy. When you are alone, you will do things you wouldn't normally do in the presence of others. An empty apartment or a parked car in a dimly lit lot provides an intimate environment where anything goes. It's a setting that allows you to relax, wind down and get comfortable. That is why group dating and long telephone conversations are the safest forms of quality time spent. However, sometimes you may just want to be alone in the physical presence of your partner. And that's fine. When these occasions occur, time should be spent in public venues or in other places that lend no time or opportunity for physical intimacy. Focus on recreational activities. For instance, museums, arcades, plays, concerts, and church service are good places. Don't put yourself in a position where you will have to compromise your values. When, where and with whom you choose to spend your time reveals your true commitment to purity. Avoid places that encourage temptation.

B) Pure Conversation

The mind is the biggest sexual organ in the human body. Once stimulated, it has the ability to trigger physical stimulation. Therefore, it is not wise to engage in conversation with very strong or subtle sexual overtones. It is fruitless to discuss the desire to fulfill sexual cravings with one another. Especially when there is a goal to abstain from physical intimacy. It only serves to tease the mind and body. Ephesians 4:29 says, *"Watch the way you talk. Let nothing foul or dirty come out of your mouth. Say only what helps, each word a gift (The Message)."* Sexually stimulating conversation is not helpful. It plants seeds of carnality that can manifest. It is beneficial to engage in conversation of a pure nature. Talk about current affairs, like interests, spiritual topics, social issues and other neutral topics that help establish a positive relationship.

175

C) Guard Your Sexual Triggers

How far is too far? This is a question that has been on the hearts, minds and lips of countless men and women who are considering a life of celibacy. While some view kissing, caressing and fondling as no big deal. Others feel it is completely inappropriate.

Though many couples have sworn to a life of abstinence until marriage, they have drawn a fine line as to what they will and will not do. Theoretically, it sounds like a pretty good plan. However, in all practicality, it is very problematic. You see, a sensual touch triggers a physiological response. So, while your mind tells you one thing, your body screams something entirely different. Although some men and women can successfully maintain a level of physical restraint for long periods of time, resentment, regret and guilt surmount from habitual acts of weakness, which carry them into forbidden territory.

Continuous visual rehearsals of sexual experiences make the possibility of having sex even easier. With such fantasies, one thing often leads to another. Which leads to another. Which leads to another. Pretty soon, temptation arises, sin occurs and intercourse is performed. The sexual experiences, which were confined to the parameters of the mind, are thoroughly conceived. Genesis 11:6 says, "...and now nothing will be restrained from them, which they have imagined to do." And to think, it can all start with a kiss.

When a man and woman's lips unite, and their tongues penetrate each other's mouth, the process of becoming one has begun. Therefore, kissing is an essential aspect of the entire sexual union. Once you start, you crave for more. Then comes a kiss on the neck, which leads to a shoulder massage. Who can forget a wet tongue in an ultra-sensitive ear that sends jolts throughout the body? Then comes the unthinkable. As he struggles to unhook the clasp of her bra from underneath her shirt, she unleashes his belt while reaching for his zipper. The next thing you know, clothes are wildly dispersed all over the room and all of their convictions are thrown right out of the window.

Well, what happened? How did this all occur? How could a tongue between his lips lead to a penis between her legs? It's simple. They were guilty of limiting sex to a simple act of penetration. They dissected the sex act into several stages in order to justify indulging in unrestrained foreplay. Sexual intimacy, including kissing, touching and penetration, should be acknowledged as a package deal. But the more any two people seek to satisfy the pleasures of their bodies, the more they cheat themselves out of a truly unique marital sexual experience. There's very little to look forward to when just about everything has been done.

Author John White clearly explains the irony of breaking the sexual experience into stages. "I know that experts used to distinguish light petting from heavy petting, and heavy petting from intercourse, but is there any moral difference between two naked people in bed petting to orgasm and another two having intercourse? Is the one act a fraction of an ounce less sinful than the other? Is it perhaps more righteous to pet with clothes on? If so, which is worse, to pet with clothes off or to have intercourse with clothes on?"

Do you see how ridiculous this is? Sex is so much more than penetration. It encompasses everything from an erotic kiss, to the caress of a body part, to penetration. So, you must be aware of your sexual triggers. A sexual trigger is anything that makes a person want to have sex. You must become aware of the subtle and not-so-subtle situations, scenarios, and circumstances that turn you on. Donna Marie Williams, author of *Sensual Celibacy*, created the following Passionmeter. She powerfully argues in her book that the sexual experience cannot be broken into various stages. Rather, it is a transitional flow from one act to another. Every sexual act performed eventually carries into another once it no longer satisfies. The following is the natural course that two people take which often ends in fornication: Talking > holding hands > eye gazing > sweet talk> kissing > tongue kissing > grinding > clothes coming off > clothes off > doing the deed. For this very reason, couples should be very careful in their dealings with one another.

Much of this activity is triggered by lust, which is an internal burning desire that can never be quenched. It's similar to lighting a fire that gets hotter and hotter the more you play with it. So, unless you want to suffer third degree burns, don't play with fire. Arsonists inappropriately use matches and go around starting fires they can't put out. Though it may be cool to help ignite a flame, there are tremendous consequences to pay. You can seriously get burned. Besides, lighting fires are illegal, and if caught, can lead to jail. Well, lighting sexual fires is immoral, and if caught, can lead to hell. The more that you resist being physically intimate with someone, the more fulfilling your marriage will be sexually.

Step #5) Separation

The last step to master as you walk down the path of sexual purity is separation. Separation has a multitude of definitions. The American Heritage College Dictionary defines it as a) to set or keep apart; b) to terminate a contractual relationship with; and c) to part company. Interestingly, holy in both Greek and Hebrew languages means to be "separated and set apart for God, consecrated and made over to Him."

As Christians it is vitally important that we carefully consider whom we dwell with. God has commissioned His people to separate unto holiness. The bible speaks of a group of people called the Nazarites, of which Samson was a member. Nazarites were people who took a vow to be set apart for God's service. As a Nazarite, one could not cut his hair, touch a dead body, or drink anything containing alcohol. As long as they remained set apart for God, the nation thrived.

Unfortunately, Samson disobeyed his lifelong vow of separation and indulged in the pleasures of Philistine women and began to worship pagan gods. By accepting these gods into his home, Samson gradually began to accept the immoral practices associated with them. Samson's act of disobedience ultimately led to his demise.

Second Corinthians 6:14-17 offers a clearly defined set of standards concerning separation. It states, *"Be ye not unequally yoked together with unbelievers…wherefore come out from among them, and be ye separate, saith the*

Lord, and touch not the unclean thing; and I will receive you...(KJV)." There is nothing in this scripture that needs to be left up for interpretation. It's pretty clear what the Lord is asking us to do. Let me share one more scripture with you before I finalize my point. Haggai 2:13-14 similarly reveals God's purpose for separation. The scripture reads as follows:

"If one carries in the skirt of his garment flesh that is holy [because it has been offered in sacrifice to God], and with his skirt or the flaps of his garment he touches bread, or pottage, or wine, or oil, or any kind of food, does what he touches become holy [dedicated to God's service exclusively]? And the priests answered. No! [Holiness is not infectious.]
Then said Haggai, If one who is [ceremonially] unclean because he has come in contact with a dead body should touch any of these articles of food, shall it be [ceremonially] unclean? And the priests answered, It shall be unclean. [Unholiness is infectious.] (AMP)"

What a powerful scripture. There is an interwoven thread of similarity that runs throughout all of these scriptures. Samson and the Nazarite people were ordered not to touch a dead body. Second Corinthians commissions us to touch no unclean thing. Finally, Haggai creatively makes mention of the contagious effects of touching a dead body. What's the point? God is saying that if we are going to truly serve him, we must separate from all dead and unclean people, places and things.

Many Christians struggle in the area of separation. They feel that they are strong enough to withstand temptation as well as negative influences. But, in the end, they often become victim to their own decisions. Just think about it. If a group of sick people stay around a healthy person long enough, can the sick catch the person's health? Absolutely not! Healthy living is a choice. It is not contagious. However, if that same healthy person is around a group of sick people long enough, there is a great possibility that he can catch their sickness. Simply put, illness is infectious.

It is only when you separate from unclean people, places and things can God really move in your life. If you are struggling with sexual sin, you can't watch sexually explicit programming, listen to sexually explicit music, continue to associate with individuals who you've been intimate with or dwell in places that may draw you back into a life of immoral sexual fulfillment. It is only when you get alone with God can He strip you, clean you and prepare you for the work that He has established in you.

PIMPIN' From The Pulpit To The Pews

There's A Spirit In The House

The Power Of A Preying Preacher

The Secret Underworld Of Homosexuality In The Church

Teen Sexuality: Is There A Virgin In The House?

Overcoming The Lust Of The Eye

Help: My Body's Yearnin' And My Flesh Is Burnin'

Killing The Spirit In The House

CHAPTER 7

KILLING THE SPIRIT IN THE HOUSE

The spirit of lust orchestrated through the worship of Baal has begun to tear the church apart. Not only has the body of Christ had to defend itself against its enemies outside the church (those who seek to persecute Christians), but it's also struggled with an enemy (Baal) within the church. It's time for the church to draw its weapons and wage spiritual warfare. No longer is it enough to win the battle, but the war must be won. The demon of lust and sexual perversion must be defeated in order for the church to grow spiritually.

Destroying Baal Worship In The Church

The body of Christ is currently in a state of emergency. Christians are dying mentally, physically and spiritually. Baal has made its way into the church because its members have mingled with the sexual affairs of the world and have brought its carnal residue back into the church. Sadly, many Christians have jumped into these practices headfirst. They have become soaked and saturated with the spirit of lust. Lifting up holy hands on Sunday and embracing lustful pleasures with the same hands throughout the week is repulsive in the sight of God.

Not only have many within the body of Christ taken on the lifestyle of carnality, they have also embraced idolism. God's first commandment is recorded in Exodus 20:3 as saying, *"You shall have no other god before me."* Christians have unknowingly worshiped Baal along with God. Every act of sexual iniquity: fornication, adultery, prostitution, abortion, masturbation, homosexuality, pornography and carnal fantasy have caused believers to slip into the practice of Baal worship. The whole philosophy of Baal worship is non-marital sex no matter what form it comes in.

God is not satisfied with the current condition of those within the body of Christ. His judgment upon the children of Israel is a foreshadowing of His judgment upon his children today. Numbers 25:1-9 gives a very detailed account of God's dealings with the disobedience of the children of Israel.

"While Israel was staying in Shittim, the men began to indulge in sexual immorality with Moabite women, who invited them to the sacrifices to their gods. The people ate and bowed down before these gods. So Israel joined in worshiping the Baal of Peor. And the Lord's anger burned against them. The Lord said to Moses, Take all the leaders of these people, kill them and expose them in broad daylight before the Lord, so that the Lord's fierce anger may turn away from Israel. So Moses said to Israel's judges, "Each of you must put to death those of your men who have joined in worshiping the Baal of Peor. Then an Israelite man brought to his family a Midianite woman right before the eyes of Moses and the whole assembly of Israel while they were weeping at the entrance to the Tent of Meeting. When Phinehas son of Eleazar, the son of Aaron, the priest, saw this, he left the assembly, took a spear in his hand and followed the Israelite into the tent. He drove the spear through both of them – through the Israelite and into the woman's body. Then the plague against the Israelite was stopped; but those who died in the plague numbered 24,000 (NIV). "

The children of Israel, during their journey through the wilderness, temporarily camped in the land of Shittim (Acacia). During their stay, the men began to engage in sexual intercourse with many of the local Moabite women. The Israelites behavior was very similar to military personnel who become familiar with native women of the land they're stationed in. Sex with the Moabite women was more than a mere physical exchange of pleasure. Rather, it was a spiritual ritualistic custom as well.

As discussed in previous chapters, all sex acts were intended to meet one purpose, the sacrificial offering of sperm from male ejaculation. The human seed was given over to Baal's demonic beings. It was believed that the god Baal would give favor and blessings of fertility, virility and harvest in exchange for ritual acts of fornication and adultery. The Israelite men rejected the Almighty God, who delivered them from Egypt, and worshipped a pagan god all for a moment of sexual pleasure. This was a great offense in the eyes of God and his anger began to fester. Not only did they defile themselves by sleeping with foreign

187

women, they began to corrupt the nation of Israel as well. God understood that the spread of immorality had to be stopped.

God spoke to Moses and told him to kill the leaders of the people and expose them in broad daylight so that the Lord's anger would turn from the Israelites. Upon receiving the command of God, Moses called upon Israel's judges and ordered them to put to death the men who have joined the Moabite women in the sexual worship of Baal.

God's reaction to the sins of His people may be viewed by some as extreme. However, the children of Israel were notorious for allowing pagan cultures to draw them away from the true purpose and presence of God, which ultimately led to their demise.

God's reaction was necessary for two reasons. First, there had to be a punishment for the sin of disobedience. God would have operated against his own law if he hadn't responded accordingly. Second, God had to keep the rest of the nation free from the contamination of Moabite culture and ritualistic worship. The spiritual cleansing God orchestrated ultimately led to the death of 24,000 Israelites. Not only were the Israelite men put to death for their sin against God, but the nation of Moab was ordered by God to be destroyed as well.

God is serious about the spiritual state of his people and is willing to do whatever is required to keep his people holy. Just as Moses ordered the judges to kill those involved in Baal worship, the leadership within the body of Christ is required to do the same. A spiritual cleansing must take place within God's house and every spiritual leader must curse and expel the spirit of Baal within their house of worship. The spirit of fornication, promiscuity, adultery and homosexuality must be exposed and expelled.

In the movie *Outbreak,* a monkey carrying a deadly disease infected a shop owner. The contamination quickly spread airborne and, within hours, infected other residents of the town. Within the course of three days, thousands of people were rapidly dying. The military was called in to quarantine the entire city to prevent the disease from spreading. Barbwire was put up all around the perimeter of the city limits. No one was allowed in or out under any circumstances. Any individual who became incompliant with such orders was shot down and killed in order to keep the disease from spreading. The spreading of the infectious disease would render death to an entire nation.

Many have been contaminated with the spirit of lust and the church has been silent for too long. As a result, many casualties have taken place. The church must begin to wage war and fight in order to, once again, reclaim its own. The bible says the weapons of our warfare are not carnal but mighty through the pulling down of strongholds. The body of Christ must adorn themselves with the full armor of God and go on a killing spree. There are countless saints within the church who carry a lustful spirit that needs to be killed. The spirit of fornication in all of its forms need to utterly be destroyed. If it is not, then that demonic spirit will spread throughout the church and kill (spiritually and physically) every believer in sight.

Therefore the church must wage war by destroying generational curses, casting demonic spirits out of the people and effectively teaching people how to overcome sexual battles through the word of God. We as believers are soldiers in the army of the Lord and it is time to kill and destroy every trick, scheme and wile of the devil.

Showdown On Mt. Carmel

The kingdom of Israel suffered a steady decline because its allegiance to God had been compromised. King Ahab, who ruled Israel for twenty-two years, was the son of a man who gained his kingship through assassination. King Ahab did more evil in the eyes of the Lord than any of those before him. He married Jezebel, the daughter of a Phoenician high priest and king. Instead of worshiping the true God, Ahab and his wife Jezebel worshiped Baal, the most popular Canaanite god. In order to please her Ahab built a temple and an altar to Baal thus promoting idolatry and leading the entire nation into sin.

Jezebel built pagan altars and murdered most of the Lord's prophets, replacing them with more than 800 occult priests, soothsayers and temple prostitutes. More than 450 prophets of Baal served Jezebel's desires. There were only one hundred of God's prophets left. As a result, Jezebel influenced millions of Israelites to forsake their covenant with God. The occult priests were active in spreading the doctrine of Idol worship and advocated pagan god worship, common among the Phoenicians and Greeks.

In the midst of Israel's decay, God raised up the prophet Elijah. Elijah was one of the great prophets crying repentance to the kings of Israel. He was angered by the political direction and the spiritual state of the nation of Israel. The children of Israel tried to follow both the Lord and Baal. Baal supposedly was the god of the rains and harvest. So, Elijah, through God's power, decided to seal the heavens and cause a great drought in the land. Elijah decreed, not one drop of rain would fall to the ground while the heavens have been sealed. The judgment decreed was a 3½ year drought in Israel. Many people suffered and died. Elijah was proving to all of Israel that Baal had no power and Israel's loyalty to it was misplaced.

The judgment quickly received the attention of King Ahab. Towards the end of the drought, the prophet Elijah then challenged Ahab. First Kings 18:19 says, *"Now bring all the people of Israel to Mount Carmel, with all 450 prophets of Baal and the 400 prophets of Asherah (sea goddess and mistress of Baal) who are supported by Jezebel (TLB)."* So Ahab ordered all of the people and prophets to appear on Mount Carmel. Elijah, the one true prophet of God, boldly faced the eight-hundred and fifty prophets alone. Elijah then questioned the people and asked how long they were going to waver between two opinions. "If the Lord is God, follow Him! But if Baal is God, then follow him!" This same question must be asked to the body of Christ. Who are you going to serve, God or Baal? You can't serve two masters.

Elijah challenged the priests of Baal to take a bull and prepare it for sacrifice to Baal and he would do the same to the almighty God. The test involved the sacrifice being consumed by fire. If Baal accepted their sacrifice and sent down fire from heaven the priests would be declared the winner and Israel would follow Baal. However, if the priests sacrifice was not accepted, Elijah would be given the chance to make a sacrifice to the God of Abraham,

191

Isaac and Jacob. If fire consumed Elijah's offering, Israel would follow the Lord.

The prophets of Baal were in a sticky situation and had no choice but to perform the sacrificial act before the people. The contest lasted all day with the four hundred fifty priests of Baal chanting, "O Baal, hear us." But there was no response, nor any voice that answered. For more than three hours they tried to invoke the aid of Baal. Elijah sat in a chair some distance away, watching with interest. The priest leaped upon the altar, cutting themselves till blood gushed out, and still Baal did not answer. The wailing and pleas for help became even louder. Well into the day they continued their Baal frenzy. But the heavens were silent as the people began to question the power of Baal.

After a day of utter failure, Elijah instructed the people to come. They eagerly crowded around him as he prepared his sacrifice. He instructed the people to fill four barrels with water and pour it over the carcass and wood. There was so much water that it filled the trenches and the wood swelled with the water. Everything was soaking wet. Then it was time for the evening sacrifice according to the traditions of the Lord of Israel, the God of Abraham, Isaac and Jacob. Elijah came near to the altar and the sacrificed bull. Everyone was watching now, including the prophets of Baal who had by now given up invoking the name of Baal.

Elijah then prayed in 1 Kings 18:36-37, *"O Lord God of Abraham, Isaac, and Israel, prove today that you are the God of Israel and that I am your servant; prove that I have done all this at your command. O Lord, answer me! Answer me so these people will know that you are God and that you have brought them back to yourself (TLB)."* Then, suddenly, fire flashed down from heaven and burned up the young bull, the wood, the stones, the dust, and even evaporated all the water in the ditch! And when the people saw it, they fell to their faces upon the ground shouting, 'Jehovah is God! Jehovah is God!'

Elijah then told the children of Israel to grab the prophets of Baal and. not let one escape. They were all seized by the people and brought to Kishon Brook and killed. Shortly after the slaughter, by the time the sun had completely set, the sky was soon black with clouds, and a heavy wind brought a terrific rainstorm. The drought had ended and the tradition of the God of Abraham, Isaac and Jacob was reestablished in the land of Israel.

The body of Christ needs bold men and women of God who are willing to confront God's people and show them the error of their ways. Those who participate in its worship should be challenged to choose what God they will serve and what lifestyle they will live. After Elijah demonstrated God's power before the people, he led them in the killing of Baal's influence in the land. Ministers must do the same. The leadership of the church, as well as its members, must come together to expel the spirit and worship of Baal in the church. If the spirit can't be expelled, the person carrying the spirit must be expelled.

The church has a responsibility to maintain the standards of morality found in God's commandments. God tells us not to judge others. But he also tells us not to tolerate flagrant sin because leaving that sin undisciplined will have a dangerous influence on other believers. The church role should be to help offenders, motivating them to repent of their sins and to return to the fellowship of the church. If all has been done and no true repentance has occurred, the church must do as the Apostle Paul advised, "Expel the wicked man from among you."

In the last days there will be a showdown between the prophets of God and those who willingly seek to do wrong. The strength of numbers and popular opinion will weigh heavy on the side of the sexual immoral, but the true prophets and people of God will win in the end.

Sex-Ed 101 In The Church

Sex has become the most discussed but least understood aspect of human life. The average person talks sex, sees sex, thinks and dreams sex, but is totally ignorant of God's purpose for sex. For too long the church has been negatively affected by the teachings of St. Augustine, one of the greatest theologians of the early church.

St. Augustine felt that sex was sinful. He felt that humans should ask God's forgiveness for even thinking about sex and should abstain whenever possible. Augustine argued that men and women who want to be righteous in God's sight should live in celibacy. Unfortunately, his understanding of sex became a standard church doctrine for which many are still feeling the effects of today. As a result, sex has become a taboo in the church. It is the least talked about but the most abused practice in the church.

The topic of sex is considered inappropriate subject matter to discuss in the church, yet nearly every book of the bible mentions sex, either directly or indirectly. From

Genesis to Revelations, the bible teaches on marital sexual bliss, fornication, adultery, pregnancy, incest, orgies, homosexuality, bestiality, masturbation, pornography, single parent mothers, pedophilia, prostitution, promiscuity, sexually transmitted diseases and all types of relationships. Believers often succumb to much of the behavior mentioned in the aforementioned list because such sexual practices have not been effectively taught in the church.

Everyone is vocal about the power, passion and pain of sex except the church. Television, radio, film and print media have forced sex down the throats of people for years. Television references sex, radio lyrically creates the atmosphere for sex, film depicts sex and print media offers the how-to for sex. Meanwhile, the church remains silent.

The school system has even had its fair share of sexual exploitation. Sex Ed, within school systems around the nation, has offered explicit lessons on sexual techniques. For instance, schools are teaching children how to use condoms and dental dams. They are also consulting children on the use of various forms of birth control. Abstinence is not a lifestyle that is included within the curriculum. Many educators worry that stressing abstinence until marriage ostracizes sexual-abuse victims who may not see themselves as virgins, gay kids who can't legally marry and children from single-parent homes. So, the sex education program presented in schools is incomplete. It doesn't offer the practical alternative of abstinence, as well as, the spiritual, moral and psychological consequences for pre-marital sex.

It is imperative that every man, woman and child know and understand God's intended purpose and function for sex. God's Word includes an abundance of information about sex. Unfortunately, for a long time, the only thing the church has preached is 'That shalt not' messages. "Don't do this" and "Don't do that" sermons have been preached from pulpits all across the nation. And the very thing church members have been told not to do, they've done. For two reasons: 1) they've never been taught why it shouldn't been done except for the mere fact that it's sin, therefore it held no real weight. 2) The more they were told not to do it (sex), the more it peaked their curiosity.

Sex Education must become one of the main thrusts in the church. In order to win souls back to Christ and keep the saved spiritually strong, the topic of sex must be thoroughly dealt with. Married Fellowships should have 'Love, Sex & Romance Retreats'. Singles should have conferences on 'Relationships, Sexuality and the Single Life'. Teens and preteens should have classes on 'Do Hormones & Holiness Mix?' Biblical books and tapes on sexuality should be available in church libraries and bookstores.

Fortunately, religious organizations are beginning to see the pressing need for faith-based sex education, with the principle that sexuality is God-given and must be controlled within the parameters of God's divine purpose. Rather than offering a litany of do's and don'ts, religious leaders are increasingly interested in helping Christians see their bodies in spiritual terms.

A growing number of churches are holding human sexuality classes, workshops and weekend retreats for Christians of all ages. Quite a few congregations have chose the fifth grade as a place to start a sex education program unto the age of maturity. It operates as a six week course which covers everything from basic anatomy, sexual development and expression, sexually transmitted diseases, homosexuality, teenage pregnancy, birth control to relationships. Most of the materials are biblical and theologically based, citing bible passages referring to the body as a gift. They teach that all Christians should have an intimate knowledge of their gift and know how to care for and cherish it.

An effective sex education ministry can help to reduce single parent households, welfare, abortions, broken hearts, emotional trauma, divorce, sexually transmitted diseases, guilt, shame, sexual baggage, insecurities, a warped view of commitment, separation from God, death and hell within the church. The church is in a state of emergency and the time for timidity is over. Those within the body of Christ who have strayed from the divine will of God still have a chance to get back in right standing with the Father before it is too late. The church must take physical and spiritual authority over Baal worship and the spirit of lust. If it does not, the saints of God will continue to die a spiritual and physical death and the moral reputation of the church will totally be destroyed.

It's Time To Get Your House In Order

Now that you have successfully killed (removed) the spirit of sexual sin from your life and have been educated on God's purpose for sex, it is time to take physical authority over some things. Once a major shift or change of any kind takes place, residue is often left behind as a reminder of one's history. Therefore, it is important to totally rid yourself of any tangible or intangible items that desire to keep you trapped in the pit of your past. God told the Israelites in Deuteronomy 7:26, *"Do not bring a detestable thing into your house or you, like it, will be set apart for destruction. Utterly abhor and detest it, for it is set apart for destruction (NIV).* God wants us to get our house in order, which will require some spring cleaning.

Spring Cleaning is a custom that many share, whereby they clean, rearrange and rid their homes of any hindering object that no longer serves a purpose. As believers grow in their walk with God, He often requires the same of us. There are specific things that must be cleansed and purged out of our lives. There must be a house cleaning. After getting rid of many of the obvious things, God may require that we let go of many of the subtle things that we possess in our lives.

Any and every reminder that draws you back into the lifestyle of sexual sin must be removed. For instance, music that contains lyrics that express sexual sin may be a hindrance to your Christian walk. Sexually explicit music videos may need to be curbed. Rated "R" movies that visually depict sexual intercourse may have to be restricted from your view. Steamy love novel or explicit magazines that embody sexual content must be put to the side. Clothing items, letters or even pictures of people you have committed sexual sin with should be discarded. Whatever it is that is holding you back should be let go.

Once you have successfully cleaned out your dwelling place, it is important that you replace it with something else. For a clean and empty house can potentially do more harm than a cluttered house. Matthew 12:43-46 clearly explains the dangers of an empty house.

"When an evil spirit comes out of a man, it goes through arid places seeking rest and does not find it. Then it says, 'I will return to the house I left.' When it arrives, it finds the house unoccupied, swept clean and put in order. Then it goes and takes with it seven other spirits more wicked than itself, and they go in and live there. And the final condition of that man is worse than the first. That is how it will be with the wicked generation."

Too many believers have found themselves right back in the same dead-end situation they fought so hard to get out of because they knew not how to stay out. After you have cleaned your house of sexual residue, you must replace it with things that are holy and acceptable to God. If you do not fill your home up with godly things, the spirit of lust and some of his closest friends will find their way back into your life.

The godly things I am referring to do not have to be tangible things. They can be intangible activities. The following is a short list of possibilities: Praying over your home for the spirit of God to reside therein; Reading scripture in your home throughout the day; Speaking the Word of God and loosing angelic forces within your house; Playing praise and worship music throughout your home in order to keep your mind on Him; Tuning into television and radio Christian programming; Obtaining ministering books and tapes that encourage your walk with Christ; and Praying and worshiping God in your house regularly. The list can go on and on. Whatever the activity and item may be, it must sanctify your home and keep you safe from the wiles of the enemy.

Final Thoughts

This nation has turned its back on God. What was once a Judeo-Christian country has become a heathen nation. Satan, the prince of darkness, has unleashed his sinister schemes and malicious motives into all of society, and darkness has become a part of the world's permanent landscape. Isaiah 60:2 says "Darkness as black as night will cover all the nations of the earth..." Fortunately, among the darkness must exist a light of hope. But, it's got to be the right light. It can't be a match light. It can't be a candle light. It can't be a pilot light, traffic light or even a bud light. It's got to be the right light.

Light represents spiritual awareness. The American Heritage College Dictionary defines light as illumination, the guiding spirit or divine presence in each person. John 1:4 says, *"In him was life, and that life was the light of men."* God is the Creator of life, and his life brings light to all mankind. In his light, we see ourselves as the sinners that we really are. However, when we follow Christ, the true Light, we can avoid walking blindly and falling into sin. He lights the path ahead of us so that we can see how to live. He removes the darkness of sin from our lives in order for the light of Christ to shine in us.

First Peter 2:9 says *"But ye are a chosen generation, a royal priesthood, an holy nation, a peculiar people; that ye should shew forth the praises of him who hath called you out of darkness into his marvelous light."* This revelatory scripture clearly states that whoever comes into the sheepfold is selected and preferred above others. He instantly becomes a member of God's royal family and endowed with power and authority. He embodies the character of a priest, set apart for God and lives according to a highly spiritual and moral code. He is also perceived by the world as unusual, odd and distinct from others.

As a chosen people, Christians are the light of the world. They are to be like a city on a mountain, glowing in the night for all the world to see. Therefore, the believer should serve as an example for the world to pattern itself after. Rather than being the reason why people run from the church, their lives should inspire people to run to the church. Christians' light must remain bright. Carnality dims the light of a Christian. Spiritual mindedness illuminates the light that shines from within. Therefore, light must not have any fellowship with darkness. A believer cannot have fellowship with God and still walk in darkness.

In fact, Ephesians 5:11 clearly states "Take no part in the unfruitful works of darkness, but instead expose them." The duty of every Christian is two-part. We must walk in the light and expose the wicked practices of darkness whether it is found in the world or the church. Many choose not to expose wickedness in the church for the sake of the church's reputation. In other words, the church's perception takes precedence over its members' salvation. When the saints of God choose not to expose the sin that lingers within the church, the world willingly volunteers.

201

There must be more preaching against sin in today's pulpits. And the churches that do voice their opposition against such lifestyles, must create a system that holds its members accountable for their behavior. If not, sin will continue to flourish among many professing believers. Perhaps, this is why the church has not been as powerful and effective as it could be in the world.

The church must denounce sexual sin and demand accountability of its leadership and laity. Christians must be accountable to the Word of God as well as God's people. We must be blameless and of good behavior. We must display integrity, honesty and have a good testimony among those who are outside the church. Jesus has charged each of us with the responsibility of confronting other professing Christians who practice sin – not only for the sake of their soul, but also to help eliminate the spread of sin's infection within the body of Christ.

This commission does not imply that we must become judgmental faultfinders seeking every trace of imperfection in fellow believers. Nor should we snoop, gossip and listen to alleged rumors. What this means is that if you personally observe or know that another believer is involved in gross sin or immorality, you have the God given duty to confront him with the truth of God's word. Matthew 18:15-17 says, " *If we observe a person who claims to be a brother, yet whose behavior is immoral and sinful, we should privately and gently confront this person with the truth of their sin, and seek to restore them to Christ through repentance.*" It's easier to bring a believer back to God with brotherly love and gentleness than with reproof and condemnation. When we expose the sins of our neighbor and help restore them back to God, we serve notice to the world that God is real and his grace is sufficient for them. In conclusion, as the light of God shines in you, let it penetrate and destroy the darkness of sexual sin in this world.

APPENDIX

SCRIPTURES ON THE FLESH

SCRIPTURES ON THE FLESH

Fornication: Sex Outside Of Marriage

If a man marries a girl, then after sleeping with her accuses her of having had premarital intercourse with another man, saying, "She was not a virgin when I married her," then the girl's father and mother shall bring the proof of her virginity to the city judges. Her father shall tell them, "I gave my daughter to this man to be his wife, and now he despises her, and has accused her of shameful things, claiming that she was not a virgin when she married; yet here is the proof.' And they shall spread the garment before the judges. The judges shall sentence the man to be whipped, and fine him one hundred dollars to be given to the girl's father, for he has falsely accused a virgin of Israel. She shall remain his wife and he may never divorce her. But if the man's accusations are true, and she was not a virgin, the judges shall take the girl to the door of her father's home where the men of the city shall stone her to death. She has defiled Israel by flagrant crime, being a prostitute while living at home with her parents; and such evil must be cleansed from among you.

Deuteronomy 22:13-21 (TLB)

I found something more bitter than death – the woman who is like a trap. The love she offers you will catch you like a net, and her arms around you will hold you like a chain. A man who pleases God can get away, but she will catch the sinner.

Ecclesiastes 7:26 (GNT)

For out of the heart proceed evil thoughts, murders, adulteries, fornications, thefts, false witness, blasphemies:

Matthew 15:19 (KJV)

If your hand does wrong, cut it off. Better live forever with one hand than be thrown into the unquenchable fires of hell with two! If your foot carries you toward evil, cut it off! Better be lame and live forever than have two feet carry you to hell! And if your eye is sinful, gouge it out. Better enter the Kingdom of God half blind than have two eyes and see the fires of hell, where the worm never dies, and the fire never goes out – where all are salted with fire.

Mark 9:43-49 (TLB)

Likewise reckon ye also yourselves to be dead indeed unto sin, but alive unto God through Jesus Christ our Lord. Let not sin therefore reign in your mortal body, that ye should obey it in the lusts therefore. For sin shall not have dominion over you: for ye are not under the law, but under grace. But put ye on the Lord Jesus Christ, and make not provision for the flesh, to fulfill the lusts thereof.

Romans 6:11,12,14 (KJV)

I speak after the manner of men because of the infirmity of your flesh: for as ye have yielded your members servants to uncleanness and to iniquity unto iniquity even so now yield your members servants to righteousness unto holiness.

Romans 6:19 (KJV)

For I know that in me (that is, in my flesh,) dwelleth no good thing: for to will is present with me; but how to perform that which is good I find not. For the good that I would I do not; but the evil which I would not, that I do. Now if I do that I would not, it is no more I that do it, but sin that dwelleth in me. I find then a law, that when I would do good, evil is present with me. For I delight in the law of God after the inward man: but I see another law in my members, warring against the law of my mind, and bringing me into captivity to the law of sin which is in my members. O wretched man that I am! Who shall deliver me from the body of this death?

Romans 7:18-24 (KJV)

So now we can obey God's laws if we follow after the Holy Spirit and no longer obey the old evil nature within us. Those who let themselves be controlled by their lower natures live only to please themselves, but those who follow after the Holy Spirit find themselves doing those things that please God. Following after the Holy Spirit leads to life and peace, but following after the old nature leads to death, because the old sinful nature within us is against God. It never did obey God's laws and it never will. That's why those who are still under the control of their old sinful selves, bent on following their old evil desires, can never please God.

Romans 8:4-8 (TLB)

So, dear brothers, you have no obligations whatever to your old sinful nature to do what it begs you to do. For if you keep on following it you are lost and will perish, but if through the power of the Holy Spirit you crush it and its evil deeds, you shall live. For all who are led by the Spirit of God are sons of God.

Romans 8:12-14 (TLB)

And So, Dear brothers, I plead with you to give your bodies to God. Let them be a living sacrifice, holy – the kind he can accept. When you think of what he has done for you, is this too much to ask? Don't copy the behavior and customs of this world, but be a new and different person with a fresh newness in all you do and think. Then you will learn from your own experience how his ways will really satisfy you.

Romans 12:1-2 (TLB)

Don't spend your time in wild parties and getting drunk or in adultery and lust, or fighting, or jealousy. But ask the Lord Jesus Christ to help you live as you should, and don't make plans to enjoy evil.

Romans 13:13-14 (TLB)

What I meant was that you are not to keep company with anyone who claims to be a brother Christian but indulges in sexual sins, or is greedy, or is a swindler, or worship idols, or is a drunkard, or abusive. Don't even eat lunch with such a person.

1 Corinthians 5:11 (TLB)

Those who live immoral lives, who are idol worshippers, adulterers or homosexuals – will have no share in his kingdom.

1 Corinthians 6:10 (TLB)

...But sexual sin is never right: our bodies were not made for that, but for the Lord, and the Lord wants to fill our bodies with himself.

1 Corinthians 6:13 (TLB)

Don't you realize that your bodies are actually parts and members of Christ? So should I take part of Christ and join him to a prostitute? Never! And don't you know that if a man joins himself to a prostitute she becomes a part of him and he becomes a part of her? For God tells us in the Scripture that in his sight the two become one person. But if you give yourself to the Lord, you and Christ are joined together as one person. That is why I say to run from sex sin. No other sin affects the body as this one does. When you sin this sin it is against your own body. Haven't you yet learned that your body is the home of the Holy Spirit God gave you, and that he lives within you? Your own body does not belong to you. for God has bought you with a great price. So use every part of your body to give glory back to God, because he owns it.

1 Corinthians 6:15-20 (TLB)

Nevertheless, to avoid fornication, let every man have his own wife, and let every woman have her own husband.

1 Corinthians 7:2 (KJV)

So I say to those who aren't married, and to widows – better to stay unmarried if you can, just as I am. But if you can't control yourselves, go ahead and marry. It is better to marry than to burn with lust.

1 Corinthians 7:8-9 (TLB)

Neither let us commit fornication, as some of them committed, and fell in one day three and twenty thousand.

1 Corinthians 10:8 (KJV)

Yes, I am afraid that when I come God will humble me before you and I will be sad and mourn because many of you who have sinned became sinners and don't even care about the wicked, impure things you have done: your lust and immorality, and the taking of other men's wives.

2 Corinthians 12:21 (TLB)

Walk in the Spirit, and ye shall not fulfill the lust of the flesh. For the flesh lusteth against the Spirit, and the Spirit against the flesh: and these are contrary the one to the other: so that ye cannot do the things that ye would....Now the works of the flesh are manifest, which are these; Adultery, fornication, uncleanness, lasciviousness...as I have told you in time past, that they which do such things shall not inherit the kingdom of God...And they that are

Christ's have crucified the flesh with the affections and lusts. If we live in the Spirit, let us also walk in the Spirit.

Galatians 5:16-25 (KJV)

For he that soweth to his flesh shall of the flesh reap corruption: but he that soweth to the Spirit shall of the Spirit reap life everlasting.

Galatians 6:8 (KJV)

...we all had our conversation in times past in the lust of our flesh, fulfilling the desires of the flesh and of the mind; and were by nature the children of wrath, even as others. But God, who is rich in mercy, for his great love wherewith he loved us, Even when we were dead in sins, hath quickened us together with Christ, (by grace ye are saved;) And hath raised us up together, and made us sit together in heavenly places in Christ Jesus.

Ephesians 2:3-6 (KJV)

But fornication, and all uncleanness, or covetousness, let it not be once named among you, as becometh saints.

Ephesians 5:3 (KJV)

Mortify therefore your members which are upon the earth; fornication, uncleanness, inordinate affection, evil concupiscence, and covetousness, which is idolatry: For which things' sake the wrath of God cometh on the children of disobedience.

Colossians 3:5,6 (KJV)

For God wants you to be holy and pure, and to keep clear of all sexual sin so that each of you will marry in holiness and honor – not in lustful passion as the heathen do, in their ignorance of God and his ways.

1 Thessalonians 4:3-5 (TLB)

For God hath not called us unto uncleanness, but unto holiness.

1 Thessalonians 4:7 (KJV)

If a man therefore purge himself from these, he shall be a vessel unto honour, sanctified and meet for the master's use and prepared unto every good work. Flee also youthful lusts: but follow righteousness, faith, charity, peace, with them that call on the Lord out of a pure heart.

2 Timothy 2:21,22 (KJV)

For the grace of God that bringeth salvation hath appeared to all men, Teaching us that, denying ungodliness and worldly lusts, we should live soberly, righteously, and godly, in the present world;

Titus 2:11,12 (KJV)

Marriage is honourable in all, and the bed undefiled: but whoremongers and adulterers God will judge.

Hebrews 13:4 (KJV)

Let no man say when he is tempted, I am tempted of God: for God cannot be tempted with evil, neither tempteth he any man: But every man is tempted, when he is drawn away of his own lust, and enticed. Then when the lust hath conceived, it bringeth forth sin: and sin, when it is finished bringeth forth death.

James 1:13-15 (KJV)

From whence come wars and fightings among you? Come they not hence, even of your lusts that war in your members? Ye lust, and have not: ye kill, and desire to have, and cannot obtain: ye fight and war, yet ye have not, because ye ask not. Ye ask, and receive not, because ye ask amiss, that ye not that the friendship of the world is enmity with God? Whosoever therefore will be a friend of the world is the enemy of God.

James 4:1-4 (KJV)

As obedient children, not fashioning yourselves according to the former lusts in your ignorance: But as he which hath called you is holy, so be ye holy in all manner of conversation; Because it is written, Be ye holy; for I am holy.

1 Peter 1:14-16 (KJV)

For remember, when your body suffers, sin loses its power, and you won't be spending the rest of your life chasing after evil desires, but will be anxious to do the will of God. You have had enough in the past of the evil things the godless enjoy – sex sin, lust, getting drunk, wild parties, drinking bouts, and the worship of idols, and other terrible sins.

1 Peter 4:1-3 (TLB)

215

Whereby are given unto us exceeding great and precious promises: that by these ye might be partakers of the divine nature, having escaped the corruption that is in the world through lust.

2 Peter 1:4 (KJV)

For all that is in the world, the lust of the flesh, and the lust of the eyes, and the pride of life, is not of the Father, but is of the world. And the world passeth away, and the lust thereof: but he that doeth the will of God abideth for ever.

1 John 2:16,17 (KJV)

Adultery: Extra-marital Sex

Thou shalt not commit adultery.

Exodus 20:14 (KJV)

If a man commits adultery with another man's wife – with the wife of his neighbor – both the adulterer and the adulteress must be put to death.

Leviticus 20:10 (NIV)

To keep thee from the evil woman, from the flattery of the tongue of a strange woman. Lust not after her beauty in thine heart; neither let her take thee with her eyelids. For by means of a whorish woman a man is brought to a piece of bread: and the adulteress will hunt for the precious life. Can a man take fire in his bosom, and his clothes not be burned?

Proverbs 6:24-27 (KJV)

...You have been worse than a prostitute, so eager for sin that you have not even charged for your love! Yes, you are an adulterous wife who lives with other men instead of her own husband. Prostitutes charge for their services – men pay with many gifts. But not you, you give them gifts, bribing them to come to you! So you are different from other prostitutes. But you had to pay them, for no one wanted you.

Ezekiel 16:31-34 (TLB)

Ye have heard that it was said by them of old time, Thou shalt not commit adultery: But I say unto you, That whosoever looketh on a woman to lust after her hath committed adultery with her already in his heart. And if thy right eye offend thee, pluck it out, and cast it from thee: for it is profitable for thee that one of thy members should perish, and not that thy whole body should be cast into hell.

Matthew 5:27-30 (KJV)

And I say unto you, whosoever shall put away his wife, except it be for fornication, and shall marry another, committeth adultery: and whoso marrieth her which is put away doth commit adultery.

Matthew 19:9 (KJV)

So then if, while her husband liveth, she be married to another man, she shall be called an adulteress: but if her husband be dead, she is free from that law; so that she is no adulteress, though she be married to another man.

Romans 7:3 (KJV)

Do you not know that the wicked will not inherit the kingdom of God? Do not be deceived: Neither the sexually immoral nor idolaters nor adulterers nor male prostitutes nor homosexual offenders.

1 Corinthians 6:9 (NIV)

Now the works of the flesh are manifest, which are these; Adultery, fornication, uncleanness, lasciviousness.

Galatians 5:19 (KJV)

Honor your marriage and its vows, and be pure; for God will surely punish all those who are immoral or commit adultery.

Hebrews 13:4 (TLB)

Having eyes full of adultery, and that cannot cease from sin; beguiling unstable souls: an heart they have exercised with covetous practices; cursed children:

2 Peter 2:1 (KJV)

Bestiality: Sex With Animals

Whosoever lieth with a beast shall surely be put to death.

Exodus 22:19 (KJV)

Neither shalt thou lie with any beast to defile thyself therewith: neither shall any woman stand before a beast to lie down thereto: it is confusion.

Leviticus 18:23 (KJV)

And if an man lie with a beast, he shall surely be put to death: and ye shall slay the beast. And if a woman approach unto any beast, and lie down thereto, thou shalt kill the woman, and the beast: they shall surely be put to death; their blood shall be upon them.

Leviticus 20:15-16 (KJV)

Cursed be he that lieth with any manner of beast. And all the people shall say, Amen.

Deuteronomy 27:21 (KJV)

Incest: Sex Between Family Members

Afterwards Lot left Zoar, fearful of the people there, and went to live in a cave in the mountains with his two daughters. One day the older girl said to her sister, "There isn't a man anywhere in this entire area that our father would let us marry. And our father will soon be too old for having children. Come, let's fill him with wine and then we will sleep with him, so that our clan will not come to an end." So they got him drunk that night, and the older girl went in and had sexual intercourse with her father; but he was unaware of her lying down or getting up again. The next morning she said to her younger sister, "I slept with my father last night. Let's fill him with wine again tonight,

219

and you go in and lie with him, so that our family line will continue," So they got him drunk again that night, and the younger girl went in and lay with him, and, as before, he didn't know that anyone was there. And so it was that both girls became pregnant from their father. The older girl's baby was named Moab; he became the ancestor of the nation of the Moabites. The name of the younger girl's baby was Benammi; he became the ancestor of the nation of the Ammonites.

Genesis 19:30-38 (TLB)

The Lord gave the following regulations. Do not have sexual intercourse with any of your relatives. Do not disgrace your father by having intercourse with your mother... Do not have intercourse with your sister or your half sister, whether or not she was brought up in the same house with you. Do not have intercourse with your granddaughter; that would be a disgrace to you. do not have intercourse with a stepsister; she, too, is your sister, Do not have intercourse with an aunt, whether she is your father's sister or your mother's sister. Do not have intercourse with your uncle's wife; she, too, is your aunt. Do not have intercourse with your daughter-in-law or with your brother's wife. Do not have intercourse with the daughter or granddaughter of a woman with whom you have had intercourse; they may be related to you, and that would be incest. Do not take your wife's sister as one of your wives, as long as your wife is living. Do not have intercourse with a woman during her monthly period, because she is ritually unclean. Do not have intercourse with another man's wife; that would make you ritually unclean.

Leviticus 18:6-20 (GNT)

As for the Gentile Christians, we aren't asking them to follow these Jewish customs at all – except for the ones we wrote to them about: not to eat food offered to idols, not to eat unbled meat from strangled animals, and not to commit fornication.

Acts 21:25 (TLB)

Everyone is talking about the terrible thing that has happened there among you, something so evil that even the heathen don't do it: you have a man in your church who is living in sin with his father's wife. And are you still so conceited, so "spiritual"? Why aren't you mourning in sorrow and shame, and seeing to it that this man is removed from your membership?...You are to call a meeting of the church – and the power of the Lord Jesus will be with you as you meet, and I will be there in spirit – and cast out this man from the fellowship of the church and into Satan's hands, to punish him, in the hope that his soul will be saved when our Lord Jesus Christ returns.

1 Corinthians 5:1-5 (TLB)

Homosexual Behavior: Same Sex Intercourse

That evening the two angels came to the entrance of the city of Sodom, and Lot was sitting there as they arrived. When he saw them he stood up to meet them, and

221

welcomed them. "Sirs," he said, "come to my home as my guests for the night; you can get up as early as you like and be on your way again." "Oh, no thanks," they said, "we'll just stretch out here along the street."

But he was very urgent, until at last they went home with him, and he set a great feast before them, complete with freshly baked unleavened bread. After the meal, as they were preparing to retire for the night, the men of the city – yes, Sodomites, young and old from all over the city – surrounded the house and shouted to Lot, "Bring out those men to us so we can rape them."

Lot stepped outside to talk to them, shutting the door behind him. "Please, fellows," he begged, "don't do such a wicked thing. Look – I have two virgin daughters, and I'll surrender them to you to do with as you wish. But leave these men alone, for they are under my protection."

"Stand back," they yelled. "Who do you think you are? We let this fellow settle among us and now he tries to tell us what to do! We'll deal with you far worse than with those other men." And they lunged at Lot and began breaking down the door. But the two men reached out and pulled Lot in and bolted the door, and temporarily blinded the men of Sodom so that they couldn't find the door.

"What relatives do you have here in the city?" the men asked. "Get them out of this place – sons-in-law, sons, daughters, or anyone else. For we will destroy the city completely. The stench of the place has reached to heaven and God has sent us to destroy it." So Lot rushed out to tell his daughters' fiancés, "Quick, get out of the city, for the Lord is going to destroy it." But the young men looked at him as though he had lost his senses.

At dawn the next morning the angels became urgent. "Hurry," they said to Lot, "take your wife and your two daughters who are here and get out while you can, or you will be caught in the destruction of the city." When Lot still hesitated, the angels seized his hand and the hands of his wife and two daughters and rushed them to safety, outside the city, for the Lord was merciful.

"Flee for your lives," the angels told him. "And don't look back. Escape to the mountains. Don't stay down here on the plain or you will die." Oh no, sirs, please," Lot begged, "since you've been so kind to me and saved my life, and you've granted me such mercy, let me flee to that little village over there instead of into the mountains, for I fear disaster in the mountain. See, the village is close by and it is just a small one. Please, please, let me go there instead. Don't you see how small it is? And my life will be saved."

"All right," the angel said, "I accept your proposition and won't destroy that little city. But hurry! For I can do nothing until you are there." (From that time on that village was named Zoar, meaning "Little City.") The sun was rising as Lot reached the village. Then the Lord rained down fire and flaming tar from heaven upon Sodom and Gomorrah, and utterly destroyed them, along with the other cities and villages of the plain, eliminating all life – people, plants, and animals alike.

Genesis 19:1-25 (TLB)

Homosexuality is absolutely forbidden, for it is an enormous sin. A man shall have no sexual intercourse with any female animal, thus defiling himself; and a woman must never give herself to a male animal, to mate with it; this is a terrible perversion.

Leviticus 18:22 –23 (TLB)

If a man has sexual relations with another man, they have done a disgusting thing, and both shall be put to death. They are responsible for their own death.

Leviticus 20:13 (GNT)

No prostitutes are permitted in Israel, either men or women; you must not bring to the Lord any offering from the earnings of a prostitute or a homosexual, for both are detestable to the Lord your God.

Deuteronomy 23:17 (TLB)

So God let them go ahead into every sort of sex sin, and do whatever they wanted to – yes, vile and sinful things with each other's bodies. Instead of believing what they knew was the truth about God, they deliberately chose to believe lies…That is why God let go of them and let them do all these evil things, so that even their women turned against God's natural plan for them and indulged in sex sin with each other. And the men, instead of having a normal sex relationship with women, burned with lust for each other, men doing shameful things with other men and, as a result, getting paid within their own souls with the penalty they so richly deserved.

Romans 1:24-27 (TLB)

Don't you know that those doing such things have no share in the Kingdom of God? Don't fool yourselves. Those who live immoral lives, who are idol worshipers, adulterers or homosexuals – will have no share in his kingdom.

1 Corinthians 6:9-10 (TLB)

Those laws are good when used as God intended. But they were not made for us, whom God has saved; they are for sinners who hate God, have rebellious hearts, curse and swear, attack their fathers and mothers, and murder. Yes, these laws are made to identify as sinners all who are immoral and impure: homosexuals, kidnappers, liars, and all others who do things that contradict the glorious Good News of our blessed God, whose messenger I am.

1 Timothy 1:8-10 (TLB)

"Mental Sex" Sin: Secret Thought Life

But I say: Anyone who even looks at a woman with lust in his eye has already committed adultery with her in his heart.

Matthew 5:28 (TLB)

And then he added, "It is the thought-life that pollutes. For from within, out of men's hearts, come evil thoughts of lust, theft, murder, adultery, wanting what belongs to others, wickedness, deceit, lewdness, envy, slander, pride, and all other folly. All these vile things come from within; they are what pollute you and make you unfit for God.

Mark 7:20-23 (TLB)

The day will surely come when at God's command Jesus Christ will judge the secret lives of everyone, their inmost thoughts and motives; this is all part of God's great plan which I proclaim.

Romans 2:16 (TLB)

But anyone who believes that something he wants to do is wrong shouldn't do it. He sins if he does, for he thinks it is wrong, and so for him it is wrong. Anything that is done apart from what he feels is right is sin.

Romans 14:23 (TLB)

Submit yourselves therefore to God. Resist the devil, and he will flee from you. Draw nigh to God, and he will draw high to you. Cleanse your hands, ye sinners; and purify your hearts, ye double minded.

James 4:7,8 (KJV)

Dearly beloved, I beseech you as strangers and pilgrims, abstain from fleshly lusts, which war against the soul;

1 Peter 2:11 (KJV)

Pedophilia: Sex With Children

But if someone causes one of these little ones who believe in me to lose faith – it would be better for that man if a huge millstone were tied around his neck and he were thrown into the sea.

Mark 9:42 (TLB)

"There will always be temptations to sin," Jesus said one day to his disciples, "but woe to the man who does the tempting. If he were thrown into the sea with a huge rock tied to his neck, he would be far better off than facing the punishment in store for those who harm these little children's souls. I am warning.

Luke 17:1-3 (TLB)

Rape: Sex Forced Against The Will

"...Bring out those men to us so we can rape them."

Genesis 19:5 (TLB)

One day Dinah, Leah's daughter, went out to visit some of the neighborhood girls, but when Shechem, son of King Hamor the Hivite, saw her, he took her and raped her. He fell deeply in love with her, and tried to win her affection. Then he spoke to his father about it. "Get this girl for me," he demanded. "I want to marry her."

Word soon reached Jacob of what had happened, but his sons were out in the fields herding cattle, so he did nothing until their return. Meanwhile King Hamor, Shechem's father, went to talk with Jacob, arriving just as Jacob's sons came in from the fileds, too shocked and angry to overlook the insult, for it was an outrage against all of them.

Hamor told Jacob, "My son Shechem is truly in love with your daughter, and longs for her to be his wife. Please let him marry her. Moreover, we invite you folks to live here among us and to let your daughters marry our sons, and we will give our daughters and wives for your young men. And you shall live among us wherever you wish and carry on your business among us and become rich!"

Then Shechem address Dinah's father and brothers. "Please be kind to me and let me have her as my wife," he begged. "I will give whatever you require. No matter what dowry or gift you demand, I will pay it – only give me the girl as my wife." Her brothers then lied to Shechem and Hamor, acting dishonorably because of what Shechem had done to their sister. They said, "We couldn't possibly. For you are not circumcised. It would be a disgrace for her to marry such a man. I'll tell you what we'll do – if every man of you will be circumcised, then we will intermarry with you and live here and unite with you to become one people. Otherwise we will take her and be on our way."

Hamor and Shechem gladly agreed, and lost no time in acting upon this request, for Shechem was very much in love with Dinah, and could, he felt sure, sell the idea to the other men of the city – for he was highly respected and very popular. So Hamor and Shechem appeared before the city council and presented their request.

"Those men are our friends," they said. "Let's invite them to live here among us and ply their trade. For the land is large enough to hold them, and we can intermarry with them. But they will only consider staying here on one condition - that every one of us men be circumcised, the same as they are. But if we do this, then all they have will become ours and the land will be enriched. Come on, let's agree to this so that they will settle here among us."

So all the men agreed, and all were circumcised. But three days later, when their wounds were sore and sensitive to every move they made, two of Dinah's brothers, Simeon and Levi, took their swords, entered the city without opposition, and slaughtered every man there, including Hamor and Shechem. They rescued Dinah from Shechem's house and returned to their camp again. Then all of Jacob's sons went over and plundered the city because their sister had been there. They confiscated all the flocks and herds and donkeys – everything they could lay their hands on, both inside the city and outside in the fields, and took all the women and children, and wealth of every kind.

Then Jacob said to Levi and Simeon, "You have made me stink among all the people of his land – all the Canaanites and Perizzites. We are so few that they will come and crush us, and we will all be killed." "Should he treat our sister like a prostitute?" they retorted.

Genesis 34:1-31 (TLB)

Prince Absalom, David's son, had a beautiful sister named Tamar. And Prince Amnon (her half brother) fell desperately in love with her. Amnon became so tormented by his love for her that he became ill. He had no way of talking to her, for the girls and young men were kept strictly apart. But Amnon had a very crafty friend – his cousin Jonadab (the son of David's brother Shime-ah).

One day Jonadab said to Amnon, "What's the trouble? Why should the son of a king look so haggard morning after morning?" So Amnon told him, "I am in love with Tamar, my half sister." Well," Jonadab said, "I'll tell you what to do. Go back to bed and pretend you are sick; when your father comes to see you, ask him to let Tamar come and prepare some food for you. Tell him you'll feel better if she feeds you."

So Amnon did. And when the king came to see him, Amnon asked him for this favor – that his sister Tamar be permitted to come and cook a little something for him to eat. David agreed, and sent word to Tamar to go to Amnon's quarters and prepare some food for him. So she did, and went into his bedroom so that he could watch her mix some dough; then she baked some special bread for him. But when she set the serving tray before him, he refused to eat!

"Everyone get out of here," he told his servants; so they all left the apartment. Then he said to Tamar, "Now bring me the food again here in my bedroom and feed it to me." So Tamar took it to him. But as she was standing there before him, he grabbed her and demanded, "Come to bed with me, my darling."

"Oh, Amnon," she cried. "Don't be foolish! Don't do this to me! You know what a serious crime it is in Israel. Where could I go in my shame? And you would be called one of the greatest fools in Israel. Please, just speak to the king about it, for he will let you marry me." but he wouldn't listen to her; and since he was stronger than she, he forced her. Then suddenly his love turned to hate, and now he hated her more than he had loved her. "Get out of here!" he snarled at her. "No, no!" she cried. "To reject me now is a greater crime than the other you did to me."

But he wouldn't listen to her. He shouted for his valet and demanded, "Throw this woman out and lock the door behind her." So he put her out. She was wearing a long robe with sleeves, as was the custom in those days for virgin daughters of the king. Now she tore the robe and put ashes on her head and with her head in her hands went away crying. Her brother Absalom asked her, "Is it true that Amnon raped you? Don't be so upset, since it's all in the family anyway. It's not anything to worry about!" So Tamar lived as a desolate woman in her brother Absalom's quarters.

2 Samuel 13:2-22 (TLB)

Prayer For Sexual Purity

Father, in the name of Jesus, I come before Your throne of grace and repent of all my sexual sins. Lord, help me to be holy and pure, and keep me clear from all sexual sin. I used to live just like the rest of the world, full of sin, following the passions and desires of my sinful nature. But, now I attend to your word and hide it in my heart that I might not sin against You.

Therefore, in the name of Jesus, I hereby confess, because I am in Christ, I am a new creature. My old nature has passed away and behold all things have become new. I am no longer conformed to this world, but I am transformed by the renewing of my mind.

I will cast down imaginations and every high thing that exalts itself against the knowledge of God. I will bring into captivity every thought to the obedience of Christ. I will fix my thoughts on what is heavenly, pure and of good report.

My body is the temple of the Holy Spirit and I am not my own. I was bought with a price. So, I will daily present my body before You as a living sacrifice, holy and acceptable, which is my reasonable service. I will daily mortify my members and commit all my natural affections to You, Father. And I will walk in the Spirit, and not fulfill the lust of the flesh.

Through the power of the Holy Spirit given to me, I am an overcomer by the blood of the Lamb, and by the word of my testimony!
        In Jesus' name I pray, amen.

ABOUT THE AUTHOR

Hasani Pettiford is conference speaker and author who has been teaching on success principles, wealth creation and interpersonal relationships through the Word of God for the last seven years. In 1998, Hasani founded his own company, Success Is In Your Hands, Inc. The company provides instructional tapes and materials, seminars and personal/professional development programs aimed at individuals, companies, organizations and churches.

Hasani utilizes powerful delivery and newly emerging insights to teach, inspire and channel people to new levels of personal achievement, which will guarantee success in all areas of life – ultimately placing success in your hands.

In 2001, Hasani and his wife Danielle founded Touch & Agree Family Institute. It's an organization with the chief aim of balancing relationships between self, companions and God in order to secure the growth and stability of the family. The organization successfully changes lives and restores relationships by providing an atmosphere for personal growth and development, relational restoration and spiritual edification.

Hasani has recorded an audiocassette album and has authored three books on various topics. Write or call

Hasani Pettiford for further information on how to obtain the books and tapes you need to bring total healing to your life.

To contact the author for speaking engagements, book signings or any other event write:

Hasani Pettiford Publications
534 Mt. Pleasant Ave.
West Orange, NJ 07052

Or call: 973-676-4125

Internet Address: www.hasani.com
Email Address: info@hasani.com

Please include your testimony or help received from this book when you write. Your prayer requests are welcome.

BOOKS BY
HASANI PETTIFORD

PIMPIN' From The Pulpit To The Pews

Black Thighs, Black Guys & Bedroom Lies

Wealth Builders: An Economic Program For African-American Youth